THE TRAGIC VISION AND THE HEBREW TRADITION

OVERTURES TO BIBLICAL THEOLOGY

Editors

WALTER BRUEGGEMANN, Professor of Old Testament at Eden Theological Seminary, St. Louis, Missouri

JOHN R. DONAHUE, S.J., Professor of New Testament at the Jesuit School of Theology, Berkeley, California

THE TRAGIC VISION AND THE HEBREW TRADITION

W. LEE HUMPHREYS

FORTRESS PRESS   Philadelphia

James B. Pritchard, ed., *Ancient Near Eastern Texts: Relating to the Old Testament,* 3rd edn. with Supplement. Copyright © 1969 by Princeton University Press. Excerpts reprinted with permission of Princeton University Press.

Library of Congress Cataloging in Publication Data

Humphreys, W. Lee.
 The tragic vision and the Hebrew tradition.

 (Overtures to Biblical theology ; 18)
 Includes index.
 1. Tragic, The, in the Bible. 2. Bible. O.T.—
Criticism, interpretation, etc. I. Title. II. Series.
BS1199.T69H85 1985   221.6   85–47724
ISBN 0–8006–1542–5

1773B85   Printed in the United States of America   1–1542

To
Laurey, Laurie, and
Christopher Lee

Contents

Editor's Foreword

Recent volumes of Overtures to Biblical Theology have made it clear that the way the question is put can greatly influence the shape of the textual reading. Said another way, the identity of dialogue partners can make an enormous difference in the claim of the literature. The standard questions asked of the text have either been dogmatic, in precritical church exposition, or historical, in the high season of critical scholarship now ended. These two perspectives, in their on-going tension, have been the main candidates for determining the character of the text, the kind of disclosures the text will yield, and the kind of authority the text will claim.

It is strange and remarkable how quickly and how decisively scholarship has shifted away from these well-established questions. That, of course, is why Old Testament study in the last decade has not only been greatly disordered but also why new paradigms have emerged that permit quite fresh readings. As an editor of the Overtures series, I take some pride in the emergence of something of a modest "corpus," in the sense that several books in the series now reflect a new direction of study: *Texts of Terror* by Phyllis Trible, *A Whirlpool of Torment* by James L. Crenshaw, *The Suffering of God* by Terence E. Fretheim, and an earlier volume, *The Rendering of God in the Old Testament* by Dale Patrick. The present volume by W. Lee Humphreys belongs in this same group. Unfortunately, I must be honest and say that this body of material and the argument made by various authorities are not the result of common planning or editorial designing. But that, of course, makes the volumes all the more important, for it indicates that independently and on a broad front, scholarship concerned with theological reflection is moving in a discernible and quite fresh direction that can now be identified. The methods employed are as removed from standard historical criticism as they are from older dogmatic categories. The common perspective employed in these volumes comes instead from literary criticism and reflects a dramatic, narrative sense about the text. In various ways, these studies all consider the text as an original statement that evokes not only a new literary awareness but new theological reality as well. That is, when the literary, dramatic, narrative question is put to the text, a whole new shape for the material emerges.

This methodological perspective is, oddly enough, connected in these studies to a substantive argument. In various ways, each quite distinctive, these authors have used literary perspectives to study texts which articulate the raw, dark, dangerous, unadministered religious realities which have generally been missed, both by historical criticism and by normative theological exposition. Thus, Trible studies texts in which the reality of abused woman is presented. Crenshaw considers texts of theological rage and alienation. Fretheim reflects on the pathos and vulnerability of God. In the present volume, Humphreys considers the "flaw" of tragedy that is discernible in the historical process. The common assertion of all of these exquisite and sensitive studies is to show that, at least for some texts, conventional questions have caused us to deny and neglect the main theological claim of the text. New methods permit new substantive claims to be noticed. In each case, such a reading of the text is a great awkwardness for established religion, whether that established claim is of conventional dogmatics or of liberal rationalism that tends to go alongside historical criticism.

That this corpus of literature has emerged with such force, without common planning or editorial design, likely reflects the current cultural situation. That is, method and substance are no doubt evoked in the context of specific cultural questions. As I think all of these authors would agree, ours is peculiarly a time of abuse, rage, vulnerability, tragedy. Every interpreter is a child and mirror of her or his own interpretive setting, and that is surely the case here.

Professor Humphreys's particular contribution to this general approach grows out of his longstanding sensitivity to literary matters and his considerable reflection, especially on the Saul materials, and on the dramatic and narrative aspects of the text in general. He shows himself to be an acute observer of the subtleties of the text. That acuteness is matched by his impressive sense of the tragic tradition that conventionally has lived in great tension with the Bible, particularly when the Bible has been read in a more triumphant mode.

But Humphreys's literary analysis is peculiarly poignant precisely because he understands how powerful and odd the tragic is, given our cultural context. The technological madness, the race for security that leads toward destruction, the loss of humane categories in our satiation, the Promethean tendency among us—all this requires the handlers of the biblical tradition to see underneath, to see the awesome, hurtful truth that will not be denied by "high-tech" nor overcome by "high touch." Humphreys wisely and with discipline gives no attention to "relevance." What becomes clear is that when the texts are heard through the question of tragedy, they have their own say without any gesture of relevance. The end result is a powerful claim of authority made for these texts which is intrinsic to the material. Such an assertion of authority is enormously important when all extrinsic authority has collapsed (see Edward Farley, *Ecclesial Reflection: An Anatomy of Theological Method* [Philadelphia: Fortress Press, 1982]), and we seem to be left only with ideological posturing. In such a season as ours, the text waits quietly with its own authority. Then it does become disclosing—even revealing, for those who wait with it. That disclosure sets these texts both in a larger literary world of the tragic and in a political social setting of technological anxiety and despair. But neither the literature nor the sociology diminishes the powerful word offered here. That word speaks—about us and out beyond us. With great delicacy Humphreys brings to speech this special voice that bears its own truth among us.

WALTER BRUEGGEMANN

Preface

Elie Wiesel, in his little book called *Night,* tells of his early encounters with a man named Moche, who was the beadle in the house of study in Sighet, his home town in Transylvania. Moche became one of Elie's teachers. And what did the young Elie Wiesel learn from Moche the Beadle? "He explained to me with great insistence that every question possessed a power that did not lie in the answer."

Wiesel's book itself—his brief but powerful account of his journey into and out of the Holocaust—provokes questions that disturb in such a profound way that they are difficult even to ask. Where is God now?

The tragic vision provokes questions of this type, questions that possess a power that does not lie in the answers. The tragic vision does not constitute a faith; rather, it creates a context in which faith may fail or in which a sustained and sustaining faith can mature.

While the traditions that dominate in the Hebrew Bible provide little enough support for a sustained development of the tragic vision, the ability of that tradition to confront at critical points the potential for tragedy honed it and kept it strong. Especially in the old story of Saul, Israel's first king, and again in the poem of Job, Israel confronted the power of the tragic vision. And if in time that vision was blunted or transcended, this confrontation provides an important if neglected aspect in the story of the development of the Hebraic religious traditions.

Here we will consider the tragic vision and the powerful questions it provokes. "Tragedy" is a much used and abused term. We do not mean by it simply anything that is bad or unfortunate, however deeply it may tear at our hearts. As we will discuss in the opening chapter, tragedy and the tragic vision maintain a delicate but vital balance between what we will call fate and flaw. There are profound theological dimensions to the tragic vision. We will first try out our understanding of the tragic vision on the ancient *Gilgamesh Epic,* material that is almost always neglected when the roots of tragedy are discussed. Next we will consider an old form of the story of King Saul that underlies and shapes 1 Samuel 9—31. In it the life of Israel's first king is refracted through the tragic vision.

We will then consider ways in which more normative expressions of Israelite faith absorbed this old story into contexts that effectively blunted it as the figure of Saul was recast from tragic hero to villain. This appropriation and transformation of the tragic is important as we seek to understand the faith of Israel, for it casts a distinctive light on prophetic and royalist traditions. Then other instances in which a potential for the tragic is present are considered in what I have called "flirtations with the tragic" (see chap. 4). Their absorption into the mainstream will engage us as well. The Book of Job will engage us in chapter 5, and as a counterpoint the Book of Koheleth (Ecclesiastes) will be considered in chapter 6. In conclusion we will suggest what our review indicates, namely, that certain times and seasons seem ripe for the sustained development of the tragic vision. In ancient Israel the period of transition from federation to empire under David and Solomon and then the period of Exile following the destruction of Jerusalem in 587 B.C.E. were just such critical seasons. The possibility that we today live in such a time cannot then be avoided.

The roots of this study go back to my undergraduate days at the University of Rochester, to a remark by Professor David Hadas on the incompatibility of tragedy and Christianity. A seed was planted, but it was so deeply sown that it needed years to germinate. In the course of seminary training I was especially attracted to the material dealing with King Saul in the First Book of Samuel. This was due in large measure to the stimulation I received from Professor R. Lansing Hicks. I did not return to the material again for many years, for in graduate study I turned to other material within the Hebraic tradition. However, the debt I owe to Professors Samuel L. Terrien, James A. Sanders, and George Landes is quite likely still more extensive than I yet recognize.

I was drawn to the figure of Saul once more in the course of teaching and research as a member of the Department of Religious Studies at the University of Tennessee in Knoxville. To that institution for two Faculty Summer Research Grants, and to the National

Endowment for the Humanities for a third, I am indebted. The time made available through their generosity made not only this study but others possible. I also wish to express my deep gratitude to the students and my colleagues in the Department of Religious Studies, and especially to the past and present heads, Professors F. Stanley Lusby and Charles H. Reynolds, for their constant stimulation and support.

To Professor Walter Brueggemann I owe special thanks for his invitation to undertake this study and for his support and many insights in its production. He and the staff at Fortress Press put up with unexpected delays as I assumed new duties at the University of Tennessee.

To Mrs. Debbie Myers and to Mrs. Joan Riedl of the staff of the Department of Religious Studies, and to Mrs. Tracy Bock and others on the staff of the Learning Research Center, I am especially indebted for their skill in typing successive drafts of this monograph.

My family has ever been supportive, especially in providing a rich context for a life that puts teaching and research in proper perspective. To my wife, Laurey, and to our daughter and son, Laurie and Christopher Lee, I dedicate this book.

Abbreviations

AB	Anchor Bible
ANET	James B. Pritchard, editor, *Ancient Near Eastern Texts Relating to the Old Testament* (Princeton, N.J.: Princeton Univ. Press, 1955)
ANETSup.	James B. Pritchard, editor, *Ancient Near Eastern Texts Relating to the Old Testament:* Supplementary Volume (Princeton, N.J.: Princeton Univ. Press, 1969)
BJRL	*Bulletin of the John Rylands Library*
BZAW	Beihefte zur *Zeitschrift für die alttestamentliche Wissenschaft*
CBQ	*Catholic Biblical Quarterly*
HSM	Harvard Semitic Monographs
HUCA	*Hebrew Union College Annual*
IDB	*Interpreter's Dictionary of the Bible*
Int.	*Interpretation*
JBL	*Journal of Biblical Literature*
JSOT	*Journal for the Study of the Old Testament*
JSOTMS	*Journal for the Study of the Old Testament Monograph Series*
JSOTS	*Journal for the Study of the Old Testament* Supplementary Series
LXX	Septuagint
MT	Masoretic Text
OBT	Overtures to Biblical Theology
OTL	Old Testament Library
RSR	*Religious Studies Review*
SBLDS	Society of Biblical Literature Dissertation Series
SBT	Studies in Biblical Theology
VTSup	Supplements to *Vetus Testamentum*

CHAPTER 1

The Nature
of the Tragic Vision

It is all but universally agreed that formal tragedy is not to be found within the literary repertoire of ancient Israel and early Judaism.[1] The reasons for this may seem clear, but they have not been carefully articulated. All agree that the spare soil of ancient Greece proved more fertile ground for the development of tragedy than the hill country of southern Palestine. It is widely acknowledged that the reasons for this are to be traced to the fundamental differences in spirit between the Greek and Hebraic traditions. In the middle decades of this century, a flurry of articles and some monographs confronted the issue of the relationship between tragedy and the Christian tradition. In these discussions only slight attention was given to early Judaism and to the Hebraic roots that stand behind both. Most writing on this subject found tragedy and the Christian spirit to be incompatible,[2] although some important voices of dissent were sounded as well.[3] The Christian tradition may confront tragedy, it was generally argued, and may even nurture it to a point. But as one classic statement of the case would have it, "tragedy is not enough"[4] for Christians; movement beyond it is essential. Resurrection does not deny crucifixion, but Easter must follow and transcend the darkness of that Friday's midday and the tomb. R. B. Sewall's observation has generally held good: "In point of doctrine Christianity reverses the tragic view and makes tragedy impossible."[5]

Most of these discussions presuppose a distinction between tragedy as a literary form and a vision of the tragic.[6] The former was clearly given classical expression in Athens in the fifth and fourth centuries B.C.E. and was concisely defined at a later date by Aristotle in his *Poetics*. Aeschylus, Sophocles, and Euripides are still the "celebrated" early saints in the canons of tragedians. Their finely hewn

1

tragic form gives fullest expression to a vision that is not, however, simply confined to it. The tragic vision can inform to a greater or lesser degree a wide range of literary genres. It is with this wider vision that we are concerned in this study, and especially with its relationship to the Hebraic literary and religious traditions preserved in the Hebrew Bible. It is striking, in fact, how little has been said in depth about the Hebraic tradition from this perspective. We shall argue that there were points in the development of the Hebraic traditions in which the tragic vision manifested itself, if not in formal garb, at least as a perspective of profound potential. As we observe the degree to which this potential was realized or blunted in distinct contexts and materials, we should be able to gain important insights into the theological nature of the Hebraic traditions. A more secure base will thereby have been established for discussions of the relationship between tragedy and later Jewish and Christian traditions.

THE TRAGIC VISION

While Aristotle seemed able to give succinct definition to the tragic form and to have touched on the perspective that found expression in it, the vision of tragedy has necessarily shown itself to be elusive. We are well advised to mark at the outset of our discussion the note of caution sounded by Sewall, who suggests that the vision can be "fleeting," not easily grasped in or by all ages, that it is "not a systematic view of life" but admits "wide variations and degrees."[7]

> It is the sum of insights, intuitions, feelings, to which the words "vision" or "view" or "sense of life," however inadequate, are most readily applicable. The tragic sense of life, as Unamuno describes it, is a subphilosophy, or a prephilosophy, "more or less formulated, more or less conscious." It reaches deep down into the temperament, "not so much flowing from ideas as determining them."[8]

The roots of the tragic vision, many would assert, are found in ancient stories and rituals that lament the death of nature and anxiously seek the rebirth of life, giving expression to profoundly articulated terrors and hopes of human beings inexorably bound to a nexus of forces that sustain them even as they overpower them. In this ancient mythic heritage, in these stories that were once relived and experienced through the ever new combination of word and action, of story and ritual, moments of fleeting access are gained to a world finally beyond human comprehension and control.

Sewall himself, in spite of his well-taken cautions, provides a basis for our initial discussion of the tragic vision, and a segment of his seminal study is worth citing:

> The tragic vision is in its first phase primal, or primitive, in that it calls up out of the depths the first (and last) of all questions, the question of existence: What does it mean to be? It recalls the original terror, harking back to a world that antedates the conceptions of philosophy, the consolations of the later religions, and whatever constructions the human mind has devised to persuade itself that its universe is secure. It recalls the original un-reason, the terror of the irrational. It sees man as questioner, naked, unaccommodated, alone, facing mysterious, demonic forces in his own nature and outside, and the irreducible facts of suffering and death. Thus it is not for those who cannot live with unsolved questions or unresolved doubts, whose bent of mind would reduce the fact of evil into something else or resolve it into some larger whole.[9]

At the heart of tragic vision lies human suffering, suffering triggered in important ways by the action of the hero, yet suffering that is necessarily at the very core of the human situation in this world. In the face of this necessary suffering the hero does not remain passive. The tragic hero takes us to the limits of the human condition, driven by suffering. Life's boundary situations are confronted as the hero lives at the very edge of human power and potential, thereby defining these limits with new sharpness and enlarging all who are pulled from their safe centers by this experience.[10]

Two fundamental poles emerge in discussion of the tragic vision, defined by the concepts of *fate* and *flaw*. It has been suggested by some that tragedies can be defined by the prevalence of one or the other, leading some to speak of "tragedies of fate" and "tragedies of flaw." As evocative of tendencies in the tragic vision this distinction is of some value, in setting *Macbeth* (flaw) in perspective over against *King Lear* (fate), for example. But at best we thereby denote tendencies with these terms and not clear-cut polarities. There is, however, a danger in this way of speaking, especially if taken to imply that tragedy can and should attain one extreme or the other; for then the necessary, if complex, balance between fate and flaw will be lost, and it is precisely this balance that sustains the tragic vision.

From one perspective the tragic hero is doomed by dark forces that are captured in the term 'fate.' To be what he or she must be is ultimately impossible, for the hero is caught in a nexus of forces that thwart full human potential. To realize full human potential, to move into territories staked out by the highest human dreams and imaginations, means to move beyond limits set on human beings, limits that cannot be crossed without deep suffering and even death. The tragic hero is faced with boundaries within which she or he cannot fully live. The hero lives in a cosmos that is essentially restrictive. To be what she is and know what she must be—sister to the fallen Polynices— Antigone must fulfill the familial and religious duties placed on kin and transgress thereby the decree of the state that would deny her the right to do so. Creon and the body politic have shaped too narrow a cosmos for her to be the sister she must be; they have drawn boundaries that can only cramp and warp a person of her commitment (as a comparison with the figure of her sister, Ismeme, makes clear). To live within the decree defined by King Creon, Antigone must choose "not to be." So, too, must Oedipus, should he draw back from using all the resources at his command to seek out and punish the man who murdered Laius. As king of plague-stricken Thebes, he must do this and place himself under his curse that is a self-curse. As king he will assume the deepest obligations of the fallen king's kin:

> I say I take the son's part, just as though
> I were his son, to press the fight for him
> And see it won![11]

The irony in all this is, of course, created by the fact that Oedipus (and Antigone and even Creon) stands under a larger fate, fixed by the gods, in a curse rooted deep in his family's past. Fated from before his birth to slay his father and wed his mother, Oedipus can do no other. Behind his necessary role as king stands a darker fate that has cast him in roles he will only come in time to recognize. This gives his words truth he could never intend.

The extent to which this nexus of fate, within which the tragic hero is entrapped, remains an obscure if brutal force or to which it is depicted in sharper hues will vary. In any case we must observe that there is a distinct theological dimension to the tragic vision whether or not the overt categories used to speak of it cast it in standard religious terms. L. Michel rightly observes that tragedy "is an 'affair with the gods,' that is concerned more with Man and God than with man and man."[12] This dimension is essential for our discussion of the relationship between the tragic vision and the Hebraic tradition. We confront in tragedy a context set for human life that is not simply the result of whim or chance. The tragic hero lives in *cosmos* and not in *chaos,* in an ordered universe informed by design and subject to established patterns. The exercise of a divine omnipotence in some ordering, if obscure, pattern is not in question. The point of concern is rather the relationship of that god-fixed pattern to human values.

Order and structures are assumed, even if they are not fully apparent
to human insight. But it is an order that is not congruent with or
designed to support full human being; it is one into which human
being cannot fully fit. To borrow from biblical images (Isa. 28:20;
Amos 6:4), the cosmos is like a finely wrought ivory bed that is too
cramped or ill-designed for human beings.

This cosmos seems designed to thwart a potential that is apparent
in the best of human beings. The tragic hero confronts behind earthly
opponents an omnipotence that seems designed to bring us, or at
least the best of us, to terrible suffering and even death. In the tragic
vision the power of the gods is not called into question, but divine
goodness and justice are. In terms to which we will return, it is not the
fact of a creator that is at issue but rather the essential goodness of
creation. Patterns of benevolence, justice, and sustaining righteousness, as profound constructs of the human imagination, are called
into question and finally shown to be fundamentally inadequate for
comprehending this cosmos. Yet it is just these imaginations of the
human heart that define humanity at its best and often are at the core
of the quest of the tragic hero. Loyalty to kin, duty as king, compas-
sion for a plague-stricken city, recompense for a slain father or
children, the demands of justice: these define the actions of the tragic
hero. Their fulfillment, however, will exact a terrible price.

Thus fated, the tragic hero is flawed as well. The delicate balance of
fate with flaw, and indeed the very concept of the tragic flaw, is
difficult to sustain and can easily be misconstrued, perhaps even by
Aristotle himself. At its essence stands the recognition that the tragic
hero is active, that there is no shrinking back from before the cosmos
as designed, from the boundaries as drawn. There is no shying away
from the limits placed on human being. Heroes do not remain in
some safe center. Moreover, the decisions and actions of the tragic
hero count for something very important. The tragic hero is more
than a brute or dumb beast driven by instincts, and more than a
simple fly in the hands of malicious gods, however much that may be
the hero's perception at points. Genuine choices are made, and they
determine the course of life. The decision "not to be" is a possibility,
as Ismene makes clear by standing in marked contrast to Antigone.
And Oedipus could have heeded the cautions of Teiresias and Jocasta
as they urged him to let well enough alone. Antigone and Oedipus
chose a different route, and each decision was theirs, decisions that
defined the essential shape and quality of their lives.

This power to decide, to act in ways that make a profound difference, to exercise responsibility that is real, this tempers fate and defines the tragic vision. Without it the tragic passes over into the pathetic. Too often in our common speech the terms "tragic" and "tragedy" are used in such a loose way as to take in the pathetic, to describe blind accident or dumb chance. In no way is the impact or depth of pain evoked by the pathetic to be denied, yet we must insist on its clear distinction from the tragic. It is in this light that the concept of the hero is essential to the tragic vision. The fully tragic figure must possess stature which in traditional literature was expressed in terms of rank, size, strength, wealth; for only with full human potential is the possibility present for decisions and actions that do indeed make a profound difference. And only then does the possibility exist for a full and deep suffering as well. Not all can be heroic in these terms; not all can stand out and challenge the boundaries of life. Most mortals adapt to the limits, twist and turn to fit their bed, at least most of the time, and they can even find in it some comfort. The hero cannot and so must press against human limits in order to define his or her being.

Tragic heroes make decisions, act and live by their choices and actions in ways that make them responsible for their suffering and often their death (at times even death at their own hands). Orestes elected to return home, Antigone chose to bury her brother, Oedipus decided to press on to know: each decision was a necessary factor in the suffering and sometimes death of each. Necessary, but not sufficient. This distinction, introduced helpfully into the discussion of tragedy by R. L. Cox, informs the effort to hold fate and flaw in necessary tension.[13] The hero's flaw works hand in hand with fate to bring about a denouement that is genuinely tragic. Oedipus chose to press on, and the decision was his to make, but he also made it while under a curse rooted in his family's past, a curse that would resound through the generations of his family in the best Faulknerian manner. The course of his life was set before his birth, his fate determined that he must slay his father and wed his mother, but his decision to press on as concerned king and man of great stature raised his life and self-destruction above the pathetic and defined it as tragic.

To utilize some standard theological categories, the tragic vision seems to affirm and hold in tension both a pattern of determinism and an essential element of freedom in human being. Actions count, and choices are made in confrontation with genuine alternatives. In this we are responsible for our deeds and reap what we sow. Yet this freedom to decide and act is exercised on a larger stage on which factors and forces beyond our control, and often even beyond our understanding, govern our lives. Our freedom is neither absolute nor overall. Who and what we are is, to a significant degree, a result of decisions we have made and actions we have undertaken. Yet, in a very basic sense, who we are is beyond our control as well. The stage on which freedom is exercised is in many essentials defined for us, and it is the nature of that larger arena that is of basic concern in the tragic vision.

This necessary balance between fate and flaw points up a further difficulty in sustaining the tragic vision. This has to do with the category of *flaw* itself. Cox's insights are again useful, as he offers a critique of Aristotle on just this point: as the latter made use of the Greek *hamartia* in the characterization of the tragic hero.[14] To construe this flaw as a blunder, an error, a sin, is to shatter the tragic vision. Yet this appears to be a temptation to which all, including Aristotle himself, must fall if governed by a desire to affirm somehow a vision of a just or moral cosmos. As we have already seen, this is just the point at issue. The fall of the blunderer can be pathetic and find expression in melodrama. The suffering of the sinner can be severe but is finally just, and at best we find in its depiction the basis for a morality play. Antigone, Orestes, and Oedipus are not pathetic, and the dramas in which they are presented are not morality plays. The term hubris has been used to depict the tragic hero, and heroes do indeed seem rigid and somehow guilty in their pride, their fixed determination, especially to us lesser mortals who comprise the spiritual heirs of their chorus. Each hero dares to make his or her vision of reality absolute and then wills to live by it. Heroes create worlds of meaning and will to live by and for what they deem the good, and they ask all others, mortal and divine, to do so as well. But this imperfect world cannot bear their perfection, and the gods cannot let their vision be all-sufficient.[15] The line separating the divine and the human is threatened by their hubris, and so it must be etched anew in the suffering and destruction of those who would efface it. If their pride must be shattered by the gods, their vision of human goods nevertheless commands respect. It is often rooted in virtue and in justice that seeks the good; for it is good that they seek, and in this lies their tragedy. N. Berdyaev has said it: "The most tragic situations in life are between values which are equally noble and lofty."[16] This hubris—and the translation of the term "pride" seems sometimes less than enough—whether in the form of an inordinate pursuit of some merely finite goal, or in the suicidal aspiration toward the infinite, is not the avoidable character-defect of egotism. It is part and parcel of human nature as such, the necessary counterpart of man's creative capacity as a rational creature.[17] This is the hubris of the one who chooses "to be" rather than "not to be." The life of the tragic hero makes starkly clear the human dilemma: earthbound and finite, yet within this mortal shell having an imagination, a symbolic self, that can reach out to infinity and dream of immortality.[18]

The balance between fate and flaw may vary from work to work: from the works of Sophocles, for example, where the hand of fate seems uppermost, to those of Aeschylus, whose emphasis seems to lie on the hero's flaw. Yet the tension between fate and flaw is maintained in both, and different readings in varied settings and times lead to divergent interpretations of just this balance. Again it must be stressed that, whatever the flaw, it will arise from a nobility of character in the hero that the concept of sin and most interpretations of *hamartia* generally do not attain. There is a neatness about the working out of even harsh justice, and there is even a simple clarity in the spectacle of the pathetic, that the tragic vision shatters; for it is rooted rather in complexity, a complexity often laced with irony. There is at once a direct link and a radical disjuncture between human intent and the results obtained that provides the essence of irony. Nowhere is the irony of the tragic vision more fully attained than by Sophocles in *Oedipus Rex*. Oedipus does attain his stated goal but at a terrible cost.

What may we say of the impact of a work or spectacle of this sort on the reader or audience? Aristotle speaks of a catharsis, while others speak of a cleansing or even a freeing of the spectator. Emotions of pity and fear are said to be evoked to effect this. We shall return to this question in our concluding chapter, but a preliminary statement will be useful, one that seeks to consider the actual situation of the audience at a presentation of a classic Greek tragedy. It is commonplace to assert that for the ancient Athenian audience the effect of the drama was not the result of typical suspense about what will happen. It lay rather in knowing all too well what would happen. They knew the story beforehand; they knew how it would end, for the story was an integral part of their culture. They sat in some ways, we might suggest, in the seats of the gods for a time as they looked down from the rows in the amphitheatre upon the players below on stage. They knew what the players would only slowly and painfully discover, and they knew what that discovery would cost. They were godlike in that their knowledge was greater than that of the human beings on the stage. For a time they were omniscient, if not omnipotent. They knew from the outset that Oedipus's curse upon the murderer of the former king was a self-curse, his search for a killer a search for self-identity. It is this disjunction between their knowledge and his that produces irony. When finally Oedipus knows fully what they knew from the outset, he has been blinded by his own hand, and kingship is no longer his. The denouement comes as the knowledge of the audience and those on stage comes at last together. For a time the audience is able to be above it all, detached, observing, sympathetic, appalled even, but to a significant degree removed by their greater knowledge. For a time the audience seems able to transcend the tragic essence of human life as lived before their eyes.[19] They do not and cannot get too close to the tragic hero. Empathy is possible but not to the point of identity. Awe and respect are possible, but distance is maintained.

Then, as the play ends, the audience comes down from their place above the stage and crosses over onto the stage of their own lives. They are players now in their own limited dramas. But they have the experience of the other drama as well, knowing that, just as Orestes in his devotion, Oedipus in his search, Antigone in her determination, they too must make decisions and act, if not on so grand a scale or so near life's limits. They too must bear responsibility for their actions, while caught up as well in a nexus of forces beyond their knowledge and control. They must also act and reap the fruits of action while caught up in a larger context that can give to their decisions and actions depth and dimensions they do not intend. We in the audience may not live on the heroic scale—for by definition few can be heroic—but all can be enlarged by the drama of the suffering tragic hero who presses to the limits of human being, who dares fully to be, and that enlargement can enrich the lives of all who perceive it.

THE TRAGIC VISION AND
THE GILGAMESH EPIC

In our initial remarks about the tragic vision, we have drawn illustrative material from the formal Athenian tragedies. We have utilized the same sources with which most discussions of tragedy begin. But the tragic vision is larger than the pure forms of Greek tragedy, and it informs a wide range of literature. Before turning to the Hebraic heritage and its relationships to the tragic vision, it will prove instructive to bring our general remarks to bear on an even older piece of literature, *The Gilgamesh Epic*, a part of the heritage of the ancient Israelites themselves. This epic reveals none of the formal qualities of a drama by Sophocles; it is indeed quite picaresque. Yet it will appear that in this ancient example of Mesopotamian scribal creativity the essence of the tragic vision was defined, perhaps for the first time in human literary history.

Gilgamesh was a historical figure; he was the king of Uruk (biblical Erek) around 2600 B.C.E. While little historical record remains of his rule, he is noted in the Sumerian King List, and about him a rich lore developed. We first meet him in short accounts of his adventures produced by the scribes of the Third Dynasty of Ur (2060–1950 B.C.E.), who counted him among their illustrious ancestors. The Akkadian epic of Gilgamesh is, however, a product of the Old Babylonian Period (1830–1530 B.C.E.)—the era of the great Hammurabi. It is with this extended epic, which remained popular throughout the ancient Near East and eastern Mediterranean world for the next 1500 years, that we are here concerned.[20]

As the epic opens, we are introduced to Gilgamesh as a man cast in the heroic mode:[21]

> He who saw everything to the ends of the land,
> Who all things experienced, considered all!
>
> . . . .
>
> The hidden he saw, laid bare the undisclosed.
>
> . . . .
>
> Achieved a long journey, tiring and resting.

Singled out in this brief recounting of Gilgamesh's achievements is his city of Uruk, the magnificent walls of which he is said to have constructed and which were its pride.

> Go up and walk on the walls of Uruk,
> Inspect the base terrace, examine the brickwork:
> Is not its brickwork of burnt brick?
> Did not the Seven Sages lay its foundations?

Of Gilgamesh himself we are told not only that his mother was the goddess Ninsun but that he was of extraordinary stature and unbounded in vigor and appetite. In spite of his divine mother, he was mortal but of royal rank and position that would befit a classical hero. Indeed, his energy and appetites cannot be contained within the bounds defined by normal human decency. He has outraged the citizenry of Uruk through actions the nature of which is not wholly clear but which seem to involve his vast sexual desires. Unable to curb their king, the elders of his city appeal to the assembly of the gods for aid. This the deities attempt to give in the form of Enkidu, a wild man in some ways the equal of Gilgamesh: he should put the unbridled king in his place.

When we first meet Enkidu, he is the ancient equivalent of the "noble savage." This originally childlike creature is wholly at one with nature.[22]

> Shaggy with hair is his whole body,
>   He is endowed with head hair like a woman.
>
> . . . .
>
> He knows neither people nor land;
>
> . . . .
>
> With the gazelles he feeds on grass,
> With the wild beasts he jostles at the watering-place,
> With the teeming creatures his heart delights in water.

The contrast between the innocent and natural Enkidu, while the equal of Gilgamesh in stature, and the sophisticated and urbanized Gilgamesh is striking, providing an important theme in the first part of the epic. While at home in nature, Enkidu must come in time into contact with human beings. Having thwarted a hunter's attempt to take prey, Enkidu is introduced by the hunter to a harlot. A week-long encounter with human sexuality—he too is heroic in even this first experience—matures and civilizes him. Before he was at one with nature; now he finds contact with human beings has resulted in a deep-seated enmity between him and the animals.

> After he had had his fill of her charms,
> He set his face toward his wild beasts.
> On seeing him, Enkidu, the gazelles ran off,
> The wild beasts of the steppe drew away from his body.
> Startled was Enkidu, as his body became taut,
> His knees were motionless—for his wild beasts had gone.
> Enkidu had to slacken his pace—it was not as before.

Physically out of shape now, he has changed in other ways as well, for "now he had wisdom, broader understanding." He returns to the harlot and is told by her that he is "wise," indeed he has "become like a god," as one form of the epic has her say.

Something fundamental has been lost as this child became mature; an innocence and harmony with nature has vanished. But there are consolations awaiting Enkidu in his new world. Quickly he receives all the basic accoutrements of civilization in a long passage worth citing for its tongue-in-cheek jabs at the civilized state of humanity.

The milk of wild creatures
He was wont to suck.
Food they placed before him;
He gagged, he gaped
And he stared.
Nothing does Enkidu know
Of eating food;
To drink strong drink
He has not been taught.
The harlot opened her mouth,
Saying to Enkidu:
"Eat the food, Enkidu,
As is life's due;
Drink the strong drink, as is the custom of the land."
Enkidu ate the food,
Until he was sated;
Of strong drink he drank
Seven goblets.
Carefree became his mood and cheerful,
His heart exulted
And his face glowed.
He rubbed the shaggy growth,
The hair of his body,
Anointed himself with oil,
Became human.
He put on clothing,
He is like a groom!
He took his weapon
To chase the lions,
That shepherds might rest at night.
He caught wolves,
He captured lions,
The chief cattlemen could lie down!
Enkidu is their watchman.

Clothed, overfed and drunk, shorn of his natural hair, oiled, and well armed—this is a pointed comment on civilized human being. Working now on the side of the oppressors of his former allies, it is but a short way from the shepherd's table to the city of Gilgamesh. The two heroes meet in a titanic struggle, for Enkidu is outraged at the sexual excesses of Gilgamesh. Their match, however, ends in a draw, and the two become close friends. Having created Enkidu to put Gilgamesh in his place, the gods are now about to find they have twice the trouble on their hands, for the companions set out on a pattern of adventure that will exceed all divinely prescribed human limits and outrage the deities. Earlier, it was human mores that Gilgamesh violated; now the two will trespass upon the territory of the gods.

First, they set out to slay a monster called Humbaba, an awesome creature who guards the cedar forest of Lebanon, the private preserve of Enlil, king of the gods. After extended preparations and some hesitation on Enkidu's part, they succeed in killing Enlil's terrifying pet. As they return home, they stop to bathe in a clear stream. At this point the passionate goddess Ishtar spies Gilgamesh and is so taken with him that she bluntly propositions him. Gilgamesh rejects her with equal bluntness and a rudeness that knows not its place:

> Thou art but a brazier which goes out in the cold;
> A back door which does not keep out blast and windstorm;
> . . . .
> Pitch which soils its bearers;
> A waterskin which cuts its bearer;
> . . . .
> A shoe which pinches the foot of its owner.

He then sets forth a full recital of her former affairs, with stress placed on her fickle treatment of all earlier lovers.

All that he says may be true, but such truth from the lips of mortals hurled in the face of a deity cannot be countenanced by the gods. Ishtar seeks and wins approval from her father, Anu, to send the Bull of Heaven to earth to destroy the heroes. Again, however, the heroes prevail, as the Bull of Heaven, which represents famine, is slaughtered by them. Now Ishtar's pet is dead along with Enlil's. The goddess and her aides ascend the wall of Uruk to cry out in lament as Gilgamesh and Enkidu boast at a feast within the city. Ishtar wails as Enkidu hurls insults in her face.

> He threw the right thigh of the Bull of Heaven,
> Tossing it in her face:
> "Could I but get thee, like unto him.
> I would do unto thee.
> His entrails I would hang at thy side!"

This is too much for the gods! All human limits have been violated, and nothing will remain impossible for them unless these two are checked. It is therefore decided that Enkidu must die and that the faint protests of Shamash, the god of justice, are swept aside by the rulers of the divine assembly. The thread that binds this epic together now surfaces in the lingering death of Enkidu. Earlier, death had been treated by Gilgamesh in the heroic manner. As a fact of human existence, death was to be confronted with resolve to live fully with all might and zest, thereby ensuring that one's death will be remembered as the heroic climax of an extraordinary life. This Gilgamesh asserts when Enkidu had faltered before Humbaba:

> Who, my friend, can scale heaven?
> Only the gods live forever under the sun.
> As for mankind, numbered are their days;
> Whatever they achieve is but the wind!
> Even here thou art afraid of death.
> What of thy heroic might?
> Let me go then before thee,
> Let thy mouth call to me, "Advance, fear not!"
> Should I fall, I shall have made me a name.

Immortality for mortals is to be found only in fame, in a name that will ring down through the ages recalling valiant deeds. This is clearly a hero's code, a path for the very few. It is for those who press human limits to the breaking point and confront human life in its boundary situations.

Now Gilgamesh is forced to confront this ultimate boundary in a new and most immediate manner. His experience of Enkidu's death is intense and utterly personal. It is with a fine touch that in the epic the gods first decree Gilgamesh's death, only to reverse themselves and condemn Enkidu. In this, Gilgamesh is condemned as well, for he is now tied to Enkidu by the strongest links of intimate friendship; in Enkidu's death, a large piece of Gilgamesh must die as well. The death of the other is the death of our relationship with another, a relationship that to a greater or lesser degree defines us as social beings. Thus, Gilgamesh, as companion to Enkidu, in his own way dies as well. As his first words upon Enkidu's death state:

> When I die, shall I not be like Enkidu?
> Woe has entered my belly.
> Fearing death, I roam over the steppe.

His grief is sparked by his own fear and his experience of death in that of Enkidu. A deep-seated sense of his own mortality is thus awakened. We have but recently come to rediscover what Gilgamesh here learns.[23] No longer is death for him an abstract fact of life, contemplated from a heroic distance and allowed to pale before the bright light of fame. It is now a blunt, brutal experience of a final emptiness, a "No!" to all possibility of lasting meaning in human life. All that richly informs life—pleasure, relationships, love, hate, memory—all are absent in Enkidu's vision of the state of the dead in the nether world.

To the house which none leave who have entered it,
On the road from which there is no way back,
To the house wherein the dwellers are bereft of light,
Where dust is their fare and clay their food.
They are clothed like birds, with wings for garments,
And see no light, residing in darkness.

a oketes

And the same empty fate awaits all, high and low, rich and poor, saint
and sinner. The quality of one's brief life on earth makes no difference; one cannot avoid death nor alter what awaits one in it.

In the face of this, Enkidu's ambivalence—shown in his review of
his course of life—is revealing. On his deathbed, he assesses his
whole life. This is accomplished in a series of curses and blessings
pronounced on the major figures in it. The harlot was a critical figure,
and he first curses her to a bitter life as a worn-out and spurned
whore, only to change this into a blessing at the urging of Shamash
(who is heeded by mortals if not by gods) to the life of a high-class
prostitute for whom men will give up all they have. Was the childlike
innocence of Enkidu before maturity better than the wisdom brought
through sexual maturity and the awareness of human mortality that
came with it? New heights of enjoyment, as well as deep and abiding
friendships, came with new maturity, as Shamash justly points out.
Enkidu seems to opt for maturity but only with recognition of the
painful cost such wisdom exacts. Wisdom brings riches but also a new
knowledge of death that sours so much of life's pleasures. But is the
child's innocent existence in an eternal present—mortal but unaware
of it, fully involved only in each moment for the good or ill it holds—
a better life? The question is not relevant on one level, for once lost,
the child's eternal present can never be regained.[24]

Having shattered so many limits set on human being, Gilgamesh
must now confront this final boundary. Uncontainable as he was
before, will death contain him in the end? His values, his quests, and
not those of the gods or even other people, have guided his life. At
least until the death of Enkidu his life has been largely of his own
making. His conquest of Humbaba and his rejection of Ishtar, and
especially his words and deeds after the slaying of the Bull of Heaven,
are akin to hubris as discussed above. This is the case, even if a clear
and high morality of all his deeds is not apparent. The decision to slay
Humbaba (who is presented in a manner not at all unsympathetic as
he faces death) is arbitrary, more akin to Lear's demands on his
daughters than Orestes's vengeance, Antigone's burial of her brother,
or Oedipus's desire to save his city. The hubris of Gilgamesh is

nuanced in the direction of hamartia but remains hubris nonetheless. The rejection of Ishtar, if rude, makes sense in the light of her past fickle history. His slaughter of the Bull of Heaven, while an act of self-defense, also averts a destructive famine.

Whether the limits imposed on Gilgamesh and Enkidu up to this point are just or not, they are limits the heroes successfully transgress. Death as it takes Enkidu and confronts Gilgamesh was, however, clearly perceived as unjust. Not only in Enkidu's vision of the netherworld as the abode of the dead[25] but also in the Akkadian legend of Adapa[26] the essential unfairness of death in the eyes of the ancient Mesopotamians is underscored. Because he broke the wings of the wind one day when fishing, Adapa was summoned to appear before Enlil and the assembly of deities. Ea (Enki), the god of wisdom, fearing the loss of a devoted servant, instructs him on how to behave before the divine assembly. Told how to win favor and admonished not to accept food or drink, as it will be the food and drink of death, Adapa succeeds in following these instructions beyond all expectation. So impressed with him is Enlil that, out of standard Oriental respect for the guest, he offers Adapa the food and drink of eternal life. The obedient servant of Ea refuses it, however, and immortality for humankind is lost. In this story, death is the human lot because of one man's *obedience*, and to the god of *wisdom* at that.[27] Some deaths may be better than others, but death itself remains an arbitrary and unjust negation of all enduring meaning or significance in human life.

Gilgamesh now sets out to overcome this final limit placed on human being just as he seemed to overcome all others. He resolves to gain immortality, to wrest it from the gods or to earn it, for he cannot accept death as his lot. He determines to find an ancestor named Utnapishtim, the one mortal who was made immortal and who now resides on the island of Dilmun beyond the waters of death.[28] Even the urgings of Shamash will not deter him.

> "Gilgamesh, whither rovest thou?
> The life thou pursuest thou shalt not find."
> Gilgamesh says to him, to valiant Shamash:
> "After marching and roving over the steppe,
> Must I lay my head in the heart of the earth
> That I may sleep through all the years?"

Much less will he accept the advice of Siduri, a mortal, who suggests that life's limits are bearable if one (in the pattern of Ismene in

Sophocles's *Antigone*) can simply cast all energy into the things of the everyday.

> "Gilgamesh, whither rovest thou?
> The life thou pursuest thou shalt not find.
> When the gods created mankind,
> Death for mankind they set aside,
> Life in their own hands retaining.
> Thou, Gilgamesh, let full be thy belly,
> Make thou merry by day and by night.
> Of each day make thou a feast of rejoicing,
> Day and night dance thou and play!
> Let thy garments be sparkling fresh,
> Thy head be washed; bathe thou in water.
> Pay heed to the little one that holds on to thy hand,
> Let thy spouse delight in thy bosom!
> For this is the task of mankind!"

"Tranquilizing oneself with the trivial" is the way Kierkegaard put it. But Gilgamesh will have none of it; his life has never been lived simply on the level of the everyday. His quest will continue.

After a series of encounters, the hero reaches Utnapishtim and eagerly presses his inquiry. At this point the epic seems to have two resolutions which stand in some tension with each other. In one case, Utnapishtim relates to him the story of the great flood. In this the gods are depicted as quite arbitrary in their actions, and it is clear that Utnapishtim's gaining of immortality had little to do with his strength, skill, or wisdom and could not be repeated in another's life. Utnapishtim can offer no way for Gilgamesh to win or wrest this prize from the gods. In an apparent second ending, death is compared by Utnapishtim to sleep, and immediately the winds of sleep fan the exhausted Gilgamesh like a mist. How can one who cannot fight off sleep ward off death? Gilgamesh's seven days of sleep, underscored by telltale signs, point up the hopelessness of the situation. Yet just as Gilgamesh is to depart, at his wife's urging Utnapishtim reveals to the hero the secret of a plant that will ensure eternal rejuvenation.[29] Gilgamesh dives for the plant that grows in the waters beneath the earth and seizes it.

Now suddenly we discover that Gilgamesh has changed. He resolves to wait and partake of the prize only when he has returned home and can share it with his fellow citizens of Uruk. But this is not to be.

Gilgamesh saw a well whose water was cool.
He went down into it to bathe in the water.
A serpent snuffed the fragrance of the plant;
It came up from the water and carried off the plant.
Going back it shed its slough.

There is bitter irony in this final defeat. The Gilgamesh of old—whose appetites came first, who cared so little for his fellow citizens—would have eaten the plant immediately, and the prize would have been his. His resolution to share his triumph with others proves fatal. The terse quality of the narrative at the end simply underscores the finality of his defeat. All that is left is the return to Uruk. As the city draws into sight, Gilgamesh sings its praises in words that recall the opening hymn in honor of the city he built and over which he rules. The epic has come full circle.

But we are not simply back where we began. True, the prize of immortality is still beyond the grasp of Gilgamesh; the gods have won, as we knew they must. Yet Gilgamesh has changed. Not only was he willing to share the plant with others, but once it is lost to the serpent, he seems willing to acknowledge the limits imposed on human being and to make the most of life within them. Possibilities remain for human life, and the city symbolizes them. The city is that monument to human technology and organizing skills that is created to free human beings from an immediate dependence on nature and to underscore and facilitate human creativity and enjoyment of its fruits. Gilgamesh again points to the man-made walls of Uruk, which define this world of human organization and technological enterprise. Gilgamesh returns to his city, just as earlier the newly mature Enkidu had to leave the steppe and go to the city and Gilgamesh. Yet for Enkidu, and now for Gilgamesh, this was a journey that would end in death. And in the city death is isolated, rendered invisible, and therefore the dying lonely. The ancient Mesopotamians knew that in time their cities would themselves decay and become mounds of dried mud.[30] The city was a human symbol, the landmark of human imagination and wisdom, and it would outlast individual human lives. But it was a human symbol and would die in time as well.

I have not found *The Gilgamesh Epic* discussed in any of the studies of tragedy and the tragic vision that I have reviewed. I would argue, however, that in it we have the first literary appearance of a significant tragic vision. In this epic the fine balance between fate and flaw is attained. This is clear as we center attention on the unifying theme that binds the parts of the epic together: the quest for immortality.

Limits are placed on human life that the heroic Gilgamesh cannot accept. While we might find his early striking out against these limits rather more akin to the frustrated impulses of a child than the grand strivings of Antigone or Oedipus, a greater stature is attained by the hero in his encounter with death through the death of Enkidu. The gods decreed death for humankind, and this is affirmed by deity and mortal alike. Gilgamesh knows it on one level from the outset. The life he seeks he will not find, as Shamash and then Siduri remind him and the reader. Death is the fate set for Gilgamesh, as for all human beings; it is the final limit or boundary.

Fated, Gilgamesh nevertheless elects to challenge this fate. A genuine choice is his, for Siduri and Shamash offer him another way, the way of acceptance of the everyday, of "tranquilization." This is the way selected by most men and women in life. Ernest Becker speaks of another form of heroism, of "the plain, everyday, earthly heroism wrought by gnarled working hands [that] guides a family through hunger and disease."[31] But this is not the way for Gilgamesh. The hero suffers deeply, and the suffering is in part the result of his decision to strive against the fate of humankind, a striving that must end in defeat. From one traditional perspective in the world of ancient Mesopotamia, human beings are but servants created by the gods to perform the most menial tasks for the gods. This view informs the great creation epic called the *Enuma elish*.[32] In time human beings will wear out and die, discarded because they are of no further use. Yet human beings are not merely trudging dutifully through life, eyes on the ground before them, nor are they inert tools or dumb animals, childlike in the pattern of the innocent Enkidu. Enkidu becomes mature, a full human being—godlike, the harlot tells him, in one version of the epic. The clearest indication of this maturity is his review of his past life as he is dying. Able to stand outside of his present moment and place his life within a larger span of time and against some greater vision, able to anticipate his death and evaluate his life against some larger ideal, Enkidu demonstrates just what it is that sets humankind apart from all other creatures. In Pascal's words he is both "beast" and "angel" (cf. Psalm 8). All creatures will die, but only human beings know it and know it in relation to a larger vision of what might be. Human being is part animal; from one point of view we are a type and species of the animal world. But human being is uniquely endowed with imagination, a self, with a symbol-making power that can reach to the ends of time and space and to the heights of beauty and meaning, that can take in eternity and immortality. As dying animals we aspire to be gods. Ernest Becker, in his last and most formative study, that leaps across centuries to link up with *The Gilgamesh Epic,* puts it in this way:

> Man has a symbolic self, a creature with a name, a life history. He is a creator with a mind that soars out to speculate about atoms and infinity, who can place himself imaginatively at a point in space and contemplate bemusedly his own planet. This immense expansion, this dexterity, this ethereality, this self-consciousness gives to man literally the status of a small god in nature, as the Renaissance thinkers knew.
>
> Yet, at the same time, as the Eastern sages also knew, man is a worm and food for worms. This is the paradox: he is out of nature and hopelessly in it; he is dual, up in the stars and yet housed in a breath-gasping body that once belonged to a fish and still carries the gill-marks to prove it. His body is a material fleshy casing that is alien to him in many ways—the strangest and most repugnant way being that it aches and bleeds and will decay and die. Man is literally split in two: he has an awareness of his own splendid uniqueness in that he sticks out of nature with a towering majesty, and yet he goes back into the ground a few feet in order blindly and dumbly to rot and disappear forever. It is a terrifying dilemma to be in and to have to live with.[33]

Gilgamesh is more than a robot, more than a mindless servant accepting good and ill from the hands of master gods who appear whimsical and arbitrary.[34] And we cannot say of him that in his failure he is crushed like an animal rushing instinctively to his fate; he rises above the pathetic. The death that awaits Gilgamesh and against which he struggles is the death that awaits all human beings. The strivings of Gilgamesh are against human limitations imposed by gods who create and order this cosmos. In this is found his hubris, and initial successes bring him to believe that he will be sufficient in all he undertakes. But against the final limit he falls. In this failure he attains a stature that the ancient Mesopotamian would rarely attain, if never forget. His fall is not in the end as sudden as those of later heroes, as that of Oedipus perhaps, and a type of resolution is attained as the hero returns to sing once more of the grandeur of Uruk. Perhaps in his case the tragic vision finally gives way to an acceptance born of suffering and failure.[35]

NOTES

1. An early and interesting exception is H. M. Kallen, *The Book of Job as a Greek Tragedy Restored* (New York, 1918). Others assess Job as essentially tragic (see chap. 5 below) but then note that just for this reason it stands apart from the mainstream of the Hebraic tradition.

2. See, among others, Reinhold Niebuhr, *Beyond Tragedy* (New York: Charles Scribner's Sons, 1938); K. Jaspers, *Tragedy Is Not Enough* (Boston: Beacon Press, 1952); R. B. Sewall, *The Vision of Tragedy* (New Haven, Conn.: Yale Univ. Press, 1952) with important qualifications in chap. 5; E. LaB. Cherbonnier, "Biblical Faith and the Idea of Tragedy," in *The Tragic Vision and the Christian Faith,* ed. N. A. Scott, Jr. (New York: Association Press, 1957), 23–55; L. Michel, "The Possibility of a Christian Tragedy," in *Tragedy: Modern Essays in Criticism,* ed. L. Michel and R. B. Sewall (Englewood Cliffs, N.J.: Prentice-Hall, 1963), 210–33; Michel draws a sharp distinction between the Old Testament, where the potential for tragedy is present, and the New Testament basis for Christianity, where it is not.

3. E.g., R. L. Cox, "Tragedy and the Gospel Narratives," *The Yale Review* 57 (1968): 545–70: P. T. Roberts, "A Christian Theory of Dramatic Tragedy," in *The New Orpheus: Essays Toward a Christian Poetic,* ed. N. A. Scott, Jr. (New York: Sheed & Ward, 1964), 255–85.

4. Jaspers, *Tragedy Is Not Enough.*

5. Sewall, *Vision of Tragedy,* 50.

6. M. Krieger, *The Tragic Vision: Variations on a Theme in Literary Interpretation* (Chicago: Univ. of Chicago Press, 1960) offers a useful discussion of the distinction in chap. 1.

7. Sewall, *Vision of Tragedy,* 4.

8. Ibid.

9. Ibid., 4–5.

10. Ibid., 5, 46–49.

11. *Oedipus Rex,* trans. D. Fitts and R. Fitzgerald (New York: Harcourt Brace & Co., 1949), 14.

12. Krieger, *The Tragic Vision,* 213.

13. Cox, "Tragedy and the Gospel Narratives," 301–5.

14. Ibid., 306–8; see also M. Dixon, *Tragedy* (London, 1938), 126–39.

15. Cherbonnier, "Biblical Faith," 31–35.

16. N. Berdyaev, *The Destiny of Man* (London: Geoffrey Bles, 1948), 32. See generally Cherbonnier, "Biblical Faith," 26–29 and Michel, "Possibility," 255.

17. Cherbonnier, "Biblical Faith," 33–34.

18. See generally E. Becker, *The Denial of Death* (New York: Free Press, 1973).

19. Cherbonnier, "Biblical Faith," 37–40; Jaspers, *Tragedy Is Not Enough,* 70–76.

20. Actually, we must come down to ca. 600 B.C.E. for a reasonably complete text of this epic, preserved among the ruins of the great library collected by Ashurbanipal in Nineveh, although many fragments of diverse ages and provenances are available to supplement its reconstruction and trace its history. See T. Jacobsen, *Treasures of Darkness: A History of Mesopotamian Religion* (New Haven, Conn.: Yale Univ. Press, 1976), chap. 7, for a general introduction to the epic and a discussion of its growth. Note especially the chart on 210. A much more detailed study of the development of the epic is found in the valuable study by Jeffrey H. Tigay, *The Evolution of the Epic of Gilgamesh* (Philadelphia: Univ. of Pennsylvania Press, 1982).

21. All citations are from the translation by E. A. Speiser in *ANET.* See

also the material in *ANETSup.* An older but useful translation is that of A. Heidel, *The Gilgamesh Epic and Old Testament Parallels* (Chicago: Univ. of Chicago Press, 1946). A prose paraphrase of the epic is offered by N. K. Sandars, *The Epic of Gilgamesh* (Baltimore: Penguin Books, 1972).

22. Cf. the figure of Tarzan in popular Western lore. I would suggest that we have here an urban perspective on the world of nature, akin to that informing Genesis 2—3 and Isaiah 11. This is hardly "nature red in tooth and claw" but, rather, a domesticated vision rising from dreams of a lost innocence.

23. See the early work of E. Kübler-Ross, *On Death and Dying* and *Questions and Answers on Death and Dying* (New York: Collier Macmillan, 1969 and 1974) and Becker, *Denial of Death.*

24. Cf. Milton's treatment of Adam and Eve in *Paradise Lost.*

25. See also the unrelated twelfth tablet of *The Gilgamesh Epic, ANET,* pp. 97–99.

26. *ANET,* pp. 101–3.

27. Cf. Genesis 2—3 and the discussion below, 73–79.

28. See G. Bibby, *Looking for Dilmun* (New York: Alfred A. Knopf, 1969) for a delightful account of recent archaeological work in Bahrain, which is generally identified as Dilmun.

29. That is, immortality, contra note 227 on p. 96 of *ANET.*

30. See the so-called "Pessimistic Dialogue Between Master and Servant" in *ANET,* pp. 437–38, especially lines 80–83.

31. Becker, *Denial of Death,* 5.

32. *ANET,* pp. 60–72. A. L. Oppenheim suggests that the term *lullu* used of human being in this epic is best rendered in English as "robot." "Mesopotamian Mythology," *Orientalia* n.s. 16 (1947): 233–35.

33. Becker, *Denial of Death,* 26.

34. See also the central speaker in "The Poem of the Righteous Sufferer," in W. G. Lambert, *Babylonian Wisdom Literature* (Oxford: At the Clarendon Press, 1960), 21–62.

35. Akin to that found in *The Eumenides,* the third play of the Oresteian trilogy of Aeschylus, or in the sequel to *Oedipus Rex* called *Oedipus at Colonus,* quite likely the last play composed by Sophocles and produced after his death.

CHAPTER 2

The Tragedy
of King Saul

The figure of Saul, Israel's first king, is a definite enigma as now presented in 1 Samuel. Later interpretation of Saul—continuing, in fact, a process already begun in the development of 1 Samuel itself— has further underscored the enigmatic quality of the figure of Saul. In most instances he is presented as a villain, even as he evokes some sympathy from the interpreter, sympathy that is too often finally swallowed up in a vitriolic attack on his failures. In a minority of instances, a more complex analysis is provoked by the encounter with the figure of Saul, one that is informed in part by perceived elements of the tragic vision.[1] As will become apparent in both this chapter and the next, the enigmatic quality of Saul is in good part the result of the complex developmental history of the text of 1 Samuel. We will first seek to demonstrate that at the heart of this book stands an early depiction of Saul cast in the tragic mode. Then we will discuss how later Israelite circles, unable to accept the theological implications of the tragic vision, recast the figure of Saul from different perspectives. In this way they were able to blunt, but not wholly efface, the tragic dimensions of the earlier depiction. In the complex figure of Saul we not only meet Israel's first king but also Israel's first encounter with the tragic vision.

My own fascination with the figure of Saul goes back many years to an encounter with 1 Samuel as an undergraduate, in which I declared Saul "unbiblical." More recently, my interest in this material has led to an articulation of a distinct structure informing 1 Samuel 9—31, the chapters which deal with Saul from the reader's first encounter with him through his death, and to the isolation of an early stratum in that book that is the basis for this structure. Here I shall only summarize my earlier analysis in order to build upon it for present purposes.[2]

THE STRUCTURE OF 1 SAMUEL 9—31

As 1 Samuel is now formed, we first meet Saul only after a lengthy introduction to Samuel, the long-sought child who was devoted as an infant to Yahweh, later attendant to the old priest Eli at Shiloh, judge and savior of his people, prophetic spokesman for the deity. By Saul's first entrance on the stage of events, Samuel and his perspective are well established and tend to dominate the narrative at least through his break with Saul in chap. 15 and later in chap. 28. Furthermore, as the figure of Samuel begins to diminish after 1 Samuel 15, he is replaced by another: David the musician and warrior, the king's armorbearer, commander, and son-in-law, beloved of Jonathan and Michal, outlaw, and above all else, the king-designate. As Saul fades from the scene, David emerges, destined for greatness. Thus, throughout 1 Samuel, as the text stands, Saul is overshadowed first by the severe prophet Samuel and then by the appealing future of King David.

Yet there are moments when the figure of Saul breaks through with a force not to be denied; from his first appearance as an attractive young man in his father's service to the poignancy of his last days in the cave at Endor and on Gilboa's height, he attains a stature that cannot be dismissed. If the reader makes the effort to set aside the perspectives represented by Samuel and David and to read the account of Saul's rise and fall with as much empathy for him as possible, the strength of this first king of Israel breaks through with tragic immediacy.[3] This is facilitated by focusing on 1 Samuel 9—31, which contains the whole story of Saul.[4] For our purposes we may treat 1 Samuel 9—31 as a distinct unit.[5]

The following outline of these chapters will facilitate our discussion of them:

Introduction of Saul as a man of heroic potential (1 Sam. 9:1–2)

ACT   I: Saul becomes king over Israel (1 Samuel 9—14)
SCENE A: The first encounter with Samuel: announcement of future greatness (1 Sam. 9:3—10:16)
       B: The first constructive phase of his kingship: public acknowledgment and initial success (1 Sam. 10:17—11:15)

C: The first destructive phase: hints of disintegration (1 Samuel 13—14)

ACT   II: The disintegration of Saul and his kingship (1 Samuel 15—27)

SCENE   A: The second encounter with Samuel: announcement of divine rejection (1 Sam. 15:1—16:13)

B: The second constructive phase: David enters Saul's court and fights his wars (1 Sam. 16:14—19:10)

C: The second destructive phase: Saul's disintegration (1 Sam. 19:11—28:2)

ACT   III: The last days of King Saul (1 Samuel 28—31)

SCENE   A: The third encounter with Samuel: announcement of defeat and death (1 Sam. 28:3–25)

B: A merging of destructive and constructive phases: the death and burial of Saul (1 Samuel 29—31 and especially chap. 31)

Two overarching patterns are apparent in this outline. First, the figure of Samuel serves an introductory function in each of the three acts. Each opens with a private encounter between Samuel (as spokesman for Yahweh) and Saul in which the future is announced, a future that will take shape in the ensuing material of each act. Second, the internal development of each act is set out in a finely articulated structure: the announcement of the future by Samuel (I/A, II/A, III/A) is followed by a constructive phase (I/B, II/B, III/B) in which Saul is successful and then by a destructive phase (I/C, II/C, III/B) in which the gains just made are lost and the figure of Saul disintegrates. It must be noted that in Act III the constructive and destructive fall together for reasons to be assessed below.

In 1 Sam. 9:1–2, we are indirectly introduced to Saul through his father, and we meet Israel's future king as a man of striking physical appearance and noble pedigree (Kish is a "man of substance," a *gibbôr ḥayīl*). The attention then centers on Saul himself (in I/A as he sets out to find the lost asses of his father, only to obtain a vague promise of a kingdom). His initial meeting with Samuel, laced with ambiguity at first, climaxes in the private anointing of Saul, the announcement of signs soon confirmed, and a course set that will lead to kingship. And so it does in I/B in which, first by lot under the guidance of Samuel, Saul is publicly designated king (10:17–27). Next, in 1 Samuel 11, Saul defends the city of Jabesh-gilead, and his kingship is affirmed ("renewed" in v. 14). Then, following a somewhat

premature farewell address by Samuel, which quietly blunts the
heady success of what has happened, Saul's first encounter with the
Philistines is presented (I/C). On the whole, the encounter represents
a victory for Israel, as the Philistines are met and driven from the hill
country back to their own place. Yet the sweet savor of success for
Saul is soured both by a break with Samuel (13:7b—15a) and his own
impulsive ineptness. His ill-timed oath endangers his son and heir,
and the total rout of the enemy must come to a halt while the army
deals with the problem posed by Jonathan's violation of Saul's oath.
Furthermore, it seems that the initiative in this battle has passed from
Saul to Jonathan, and signs of destructive seeds of instability in the
figure of Saul become apparent to the discerning eye.

The seeds bear bitter fruit in Act II. A second encounter between
Samuel and Saul again sets the stage (II/A). Saul's qualified obedience to Samuel and his god in the Amalekite war leads to Saul's
rejection by deity and prophet. Saul is no longer Yahweh's designated
king. So as to underscore this reality, Yahweh through Samuel selects
a new king, bringing David onto the stage for the first time. David
soon enters Saul's court and family through his success in single
combat against the Philistine giant, and his winsome appeal steals the
hearts of almost all who meet him. In II/B the Philistines are again
checked, and Saul is able to bind the skilled David to himself as an
able aide and warrior. Friendship with Jonathan and marriage to
Michal appear to cement the ties. One cannot fail, however, to detect
discord like that in I/C.[6] Saul remains a passive figure throughout the
actual combat, unable himself to meet the giant's challenge (but at
least not impeding the action as in I/C), and the initiative is again in
the hands of another, the very one whom the reader of the text as it
now stands knows to be his divinely designated successor. Soon
everything dissolves around Saul. His jealous rage drives David from
him and into the life of an outlaw, forcing him to break his ties with
Jonathan and Michal. Obsession consumes Saul as he devotes the still
substantial authority and resources of his kingship to the pursuit and
destruction of David. In II/C attention moves from Saul to David at
points (1 Samuel 25, 27, 29—30), where David's unexpected success
only serves as a counterpoint to Saul's disintegration. Encounters
between the two men (1 Samuel 24, 26) dramatize the contrast
between the once and the future king.

Act III takes Saul from the nadir of his career to new, if ironic,
heights. Threatened once again by the Philistines who muster at
Aphek, Saul has a third meeting with the now dead Samuel through

the offices of the old medium in the depths of the cave at Endor (III/ A). Samuel's words are bitter: Saul and his sons will fall on Mount Gilboa as the forces of Israel taste defeat. So it must be. His army is routed, his sons are slain, and the wounded king takes his own life rather than fall into the hands of the enemy. The Philistines must settle for what abuse they can wreak on the fallen king in their desecration of his body. Final honors are accorded Saul, however, by the men of Jabesh-gilead, as his body is removed at night from the walls of Bethshan and buried.

AN EARLY STRATUM IN 1 SAMUEL

The finely articulated structure informing 1 Samuel 9—31 does not preclude an unevenness in the narrative at points. For instance, Samuel appears at points as a major figure recognized by all Israel (1 Sam. 10:17–27; 12; cf. 8), while elsewhere he is apparently a seer of only local repute (1 Sam. 9:2—10:16). While this is Saul's story, at points the narrative centers on Samuel (1 Samuel 12) or David (1 Samuel 25, 27, 29—30) to the total exclusion of Saul, and the pattern outlined above is fractured for a while. There also seem to be points of redundancy in the second half of the story, the clearest being the two encounters between David and Saul in 1 Samuel 24 and 26.

These and other considerations[7] have led me to the conclusion that the structure detected in 1 Samuel 9—31 is the imprint of an early narrative stratum about the rise and fall of King Saul that has later been reworked from the perspective first of prophetic and then of royalist circles. Each has recast and supplemented portions of the early narrative in terms of its own values and perspectives and through addition of material reflective of these. We will focus first on this early stratum embedded in 1 Samuel 9—31, for in it we have one of the earliest and fullest flowerings of the tragic vision found in the Hebraic tradition.

The following diagram, closely aligned with my outline of 1 Samuel 9—31 (pp. 24–25), outlines a necessarily *hypothetical reconstruction* of this early stratum.[8] At given points in the text, later recasting of the earlier material has made its recovery impossible, as is the case with 1 Samuel 15. At other points, however, especially dealing with the relationship between Saul, his family, and David, it is quite possible that older material has been replaced by later traditions and so is lost to us. And it must be recognized, of course, that the earlier stratum itself may be composed of distinct units of tradition, each with its own characteristics, history, and original life setting. Our concern here is

not with each distinct unit in terms of its own qualities but as utilized
in an extended and artfully constructed narrative about Israel's first
and doomed king that now underlines 1 Samuel 9—31.

Introduction of Saul (1 Sam. 9:1–2)

Act I:	Act II:	Act III:
Saul becomes king	Saul is rejected	Denouement
Scene A:	Scene A:	Scene A:
Saul meets Samuel (1 Sam. 9:3—10:16)	Saul meets Samuel (1 Samuel 15*)	Saul meets Samuel (1 Sam. 28:3–15, 19b–24)
Scene B:	Scene B:	
Success in battle (1 Sam. 11:1–11, 15)	Success in battle (1 Sam. 17:12, 14, 17, 23a, 24–25, 30, 48, 50, 55–58; 18:2, 20, 22–25a, 26–27)	
Scene C:	Scene C:	Scene B:
Saul's failure (1 Sam. 13:1–7a, 15b–23; 14:1–46)	Saul's failure (1 Sam. 18:6–9a; 19:1–7, 11–17; 26:1–8, 10–14a, 17–22, 25b)	Saul's suicide (1 Samuel 31)

Introduction (1 Sam. 9:1–2).   We are introduced to the hero
through his father's pedigree (9:1) and then told of his imposing
stature (9:2)—he stands quite literally head and shoulders above all
others. For the sensitive reader—in antiquity as well as now—the
caricature of Saul's physical qualities in this introduction might recall
other such caricatures and yet also stand disconcertingly apart from
some of them. We recall introductions to Joseph (Genesis 39) and
David (1 Sam. 16:18) but especially to Absalom (2 Sam. 14:25–26).
The physical qualities of the subject of each notice are described in
some manner, but unlike Joseph and David, of the ill-fated Absalom
and of Saul it is not further noted that Yahweh is with them (cf. 1
Sam. 16:18; Gen. 39:2, 3). It seems possible that sketches of this sort
represent a flexible yet clearly defined literary motif in narratives
centered on a young hero.[9] Readers cannot help but feel ill at ease
with the fact that Saul's notice most closely recalls that of Absalom
and lacks critical information supplied about David and Joseph.

Thus, even as we are introduced to this young man of such heroic potential, a discordant subtheme emerges to haunt otherwise high expectations.

Act I: Saul Becomes King

Scene A: Saul meets Samuel (1 Sam. 9:3—10:16).   Feelings of both expectation and disquietude are reinforced in the opening encounter between Saul and Samuel. The quest for lost asses nets a kingdom. The appealing young man, who is willing to heed advice and even accept money from an aide, is honored at a feast by the position assigned him at table and the choicest cut of meat. His coming is oddly anticipated. A local seer whom one might consult about lost livestock presides at the meal. Early the next day, this seer anoints Saul in private to be leader *(nāgîd)*[10] over Yahweh's people. Odd signs follow the anointing, and Saul maintains strict secrecy about the results of his encounter with Samuel (10:15). An unusual beginning for a reign, but then kingship has not been a part of the life of Yahweh's people (cf. Judges 8:22—9:57). Throughout Scene A Saul remains an appealing but passive figure, more acted upon than actor. Events seem to happen to him by chance. Or are we to say they occur through some divine purpose? His immediate needs are met and his concerns allayed, but there are hints of more to come.

Scene B: Success in battle (1 Sam. 11:1-11, 15).   All hints and hopes for great success in this young man's life seem fully justified by the end of Scene B. News of an Ammonite humiliation of the people of Jabesh-gilead reaches Saul as he returns from working the fields.[11] What was announced in private in I/A is now realized in public. Saul rallies[12] the Israelites to a successful defense of the besieged city, and on the basis of this clear demonstration of worth he is made king by the people at Gilgal as sacrifices are offered to Yahweh, and people and ruler celebrate. Samuel has played his role in I/A and is now absent (vv. 12–14 and the phrase "after Saul and Samuel" of v. 7 are secondary). Now Saul appears not simply as one acted upon but as a successful initiator of action. Perhaps 1 Sam. 11:15 may thus be viewed as a summary of a fuller account of Saul's enthronement by the people (the LXX version of this verse has the people anoint Saul). A careful reading of this unit does reveal one interlude in what is otherwise a sustained success story. Scene A depicted Samuel, on behalf of Yahweh, setting Saul apart as leader *(nāgîd)* of Israel (9:15; 10:1). Here he is made king *(wayyamlikû)* by the people. Have the Israelites and Saul here exceeded prophetic and divine commission? If so, we have here the first faint hint of a tension that will come to poison relations between Saul and Samuel.

Scene C: Saul's failure (1 Sam. 13:1–7a, 15b–23; 14:1–46). Any such tension is for the moment subdued as the Philistines now press Saul into action against them. Rather, it is Jonathan who acts. The stage is set in 1 Sam. 13:1–7a and 15b–23, and chap. 14 narrates the outcome. The Philistine garrison is overrun by Jonathan and his attendant, panic strikes the Philistine army, and the Israelites seem assured of a decisive victory. But it is not to be. While Yahweh is working on behalf of Jonathan, events seem to overtake Saul. Not only is he unaware of his son's absence from the main camp (14:17) and of the meaning of the tumult Jonathan provokes, but his attempts to learn from the deity what he should do (14:18, reading Ephod with LXX for ark of MT, cf. 14:3) are thwarted by the press of events. Then, even more damaging to Israel's fortunes, his attempt to win Yahweh's support through his oath banning the taking of nourishment until victory is complete (14:24) ironically works at cross purposes with his desires. Not only does it weaken the army of Israel (14:25, 29–30), as Jonathan makes clear, but endangers the crown prince who, unaware of the oath, earlier violated it (14:27–28). In an episode somewhat awkwardly integrated into the larger narrative, we are told that the hunger of the people made them seize livestock in the booty taken and slaughter it in a manner that risks divine wrath. Saul must move quickly to deal with this problem. Saul's attempt to recoup the larger situation by consultation once more with Yahweh is answered by a divine silence (14:36–37). In spite of Saul's efforts, Yahweh is apparently angry with people and king. When this is traced to Jonathan's violation of the oath, the king is willing to let the crown prince be executed. The army must step in to save Jonathan, whom they acknowledge as having "wrought with God this day" (14:45). Event piles upon event as the king struggles to gain some mastery of the situation and to serve his god. The decisive actor of 1 Samuel 11 is once more acted upon. The complex and somewhat apocopated literary quality of 1 Samuel 14 reflects the struggles of Saul as events slip from his control.

Scene C of Act I therefore ends in sharp contrast to Scene B. Now the people must step in to block the king's will. Before, they had

made him king and rejoiced with him. Saul has now lost control of
events and, in spite of his best efforts, is governed by them. Impulsive
attempts to keep abreast of the action stand in sharp contrast with the
earlier situation in which he was in full command, effecting just what
he wished. Jonathan moves to the center of the action. Before,
victory over the Ammonites had been total; now we are told, in a
notice that does not bode well for the future, that the Philistines
"went to their own place" (14:46). In Scenes A and B Yahweh seemed
to intend greatness and success for Saul; now the deity is silent for a
time. This divine silence is soon broken, but it foreshadows a deeper
silence that will come in time (28:6).

At first glance all seems well at the end of Act I. Saul has demonstrated his ability to defend Jabesh-gilead, and the Philistines have
been checked for the time being. But unsettling elements in the
course of events and in the character of Saul raise disquieting pre-
monitions for the future. An uneasy note has been sounded; in Act II
its tone will rise to a crescendo.

Act II: Saul Is Rejected

Scene A: Saul meets Samuel (1 Samuel 15).   This second encounter
between prophet and king is critical not only for the early stratum
dealing with the rise and fall of King Saul but, as we shall see, for the
later prophetic recasting of the material as well. The text as we have it
is, therefore, thoroughly reworked by later hands, and little can be
designated with certainty as part of the oldest layer. Yet the broad
pattern is clear. Directed by Samuel in the name of his god to
undertake an expedition to exterminate the Amalekites, to devote
them to ritual destruction (*ḥāram*), Saul apparently complies. But
some of the captured livestock were reserved, apparently for sacrifice
later, and King Agag of the Amalekites was spared, for reasons never
given. This brings a harsh rebuke from Samuel and the divine announcement that Saul has been rejected by Yahweh. In the deity's
eyes, Saul is no longer king. All protests or attempted excuses by Saul
are rudely brushed aside by the prophet.

All is not as clear as it would first appear in this critical scene! Saul
seems stunned at Samuel's rebuke, greeting him at the close of his
mission with every expectation that he has fulfilled his charge:
"Blessed be you to Yahweh; I have performed the commandment of
Yahweh" (15:13). It is only in Samuel's eyes that he has not done so.

In a compelling way, D. M. Gunn has noted the ambiguity in the divine command given to Saul by Samuel, which permits different interpretations of it by the prophet and the king.[13] The ambiguity turns on the specific meaning attributed to the command to submit the Amalekites to the ban *(ḥerem)*. As generally depicted in Hebraic tradition, this seems to denote destruction of all living beings at the time of their defeat, and this is done on the spot (Josh. 6:21; 8:24–29). Would reserving some of the livestock for later offering as sacrifice *(zebaḥ)* to Yahweh at Gilgal (where Saul was made king) come within the range of *ḥerem*? Or could this action be construed as a violation of the divine charge? In Samuel's eyes it is clearly the latter. Yet the reader is left wondering whether Saul, who considers himself within the spirit of the charge, suddenly finds a rigid interpretation of the letter of the command turned against him for reasons that are not stated. Yahweh is not happy with his king, and Samuel seizes upon a strict construction of an ambiguous charge to drive this home.

On one level, behind this ambiguity and possible conflict of interpretations of the *ḥerem,* we can identify a tension between eras in the history of Israel, and it is the fate of Saul to be trapped at this point of transition between them. This transition was not smooth; it precipitated a clash of visions of what Israel was and what constituted its relation with Yahweh. Any figure seeking to stand between these visions and mediate the transition was in real danger of being ground between them and destroyed. Such was the fate of Israel's first king. The *ḥerem* was rooted in the old order of the tribal federation, a period in which there were but limited supratribal structures or institutions uniting the largely autonomous units. Leadership was generally of but short duration and contained to the most local level. It was what had traditionally been designated as "charismatic." An immediate crisis called forth a leader—inspired, in Israel's view, by Yahweh—who met the danger and then moved back into a position in which each and every Israelite stood as vassal before the sovereign deity. Kingship radically changed all this. In time, ultimate human authority would come to reside in one man who stood above all tribes and ruled for life. In some circles this man would even receive the designation of Yahweh's "son" (e.g., 2 Sam. 7:14; Ps. 2:7). On the level of human leadership, decisions about the conduct of war, the arrangement of booty, and treatment of the defeated would increasingly be made by the king (cf. 1 Sam. 30:21–25). Yahweh's wars would become David's wars, as we shall learn.

It is in this context that the tension between Saul and Samuel can best be set. Perhaps it is already there in Samuel's designation of Saul as leader (*nāgîd;* 1 Sam. 10:1), while the people make him their king (*melek;* 1 Sam. 11:15). Decisions like those to spare Agag and permit the offering of sacrifices to Yahweh at Gilgal from booty taken in battle would later be made and effected by kings in Israel (see, e.g., 1 Sam. 30:21–25). However, they are not yet Saul's to make. Samuel and his god withhold such authority, and Saul's position is not yet so secure that he can wrest it away. In this confrontation he must yield to the authority of Samuel and seek to redeem what he can from the situation (15:24–25). Yet clearly, the larger Philistine threat that he and his people face, if not the Amalekites themselves, demands that he have the authority that would be in the hands of a *melek.* We begin to suspect that Saul is a doomed figure, trapped between eras in the history of his people, between an age passing and an age still to come, ground by the tension between them and finally destroyed. The ambiguity of the divine charge mirrors that of the age. Asked to produce results that only a *melek* could effect, he is given at best the limited power of a *nāgîd.* If this smacks of hindsight, we must here anticipate what will be developed later and note that this early story of Saul took shape, in our opinion, in the establishment of Solomon at the apex of successful rule by David's line. The audience that comprised the royal establishment in Jerusalem knew what kings were and what they could accomplish!

It was Samuel and his deity who first secretly had set Saul apart for his new role, they who now withheld from him this necessary power. Saul's collapse came not simply from destructive forces within him. He was clearly caught up in a larger nexus of forces whose direction and intent for him is at best ambiguous and quite possibly deadly. Flawed as he is, Saul appears doomed as well. Early misgivings well up with new force. The divine silence of 1 Samuel 14 will appear even more ominous now.

We must, however, note that this is not primarily a story of opposing political theories or structures. We have here the story of two men, each of whom seeks in his own way to serve his god. Their relationship is more complex than a simple antagonism would suggest. Opposed by Samuel, Saul is nevertheless closely bound to him. After a brief initial argument, the king is willing to submit to the prophet. Saul will even confess his "sin" that he might "worship Yahweh your God" (15:30—the same phrase, "your God," that earlier seemed an effective counterthrust to Samuel's charges in vv. 15, 21). All he receives in turn is a formal prophetic oracle of judgment

(15:22–23). Saul needs Samuel, and it is Samuel's god whom he seeks to serve throughout. Now Samuel and his god seem unwilling to allow this. In this regard the dynamics on which the story turns are intensely personal.

Scene B: Success in battle (1 Sam. 17:12, 14, 17, 23a, 24–25, 30, 48, 50, 55–58; 18:2, 20, 22–25a, 26–27).   Yet Saul remains king. Just as in Act I, the private designation of Saul as Yahweh's leader was only in time realized in public, so it is not immediately apparent what his rejection by Samuel will mean for him. In the course of Scene B, in which Saul once again engages the Philistines, the initial effect seems limited. David's success against the Philistine giant brings him quickly to Saul's attention and into his court; the emphasis on the valor of David is paralleled by Saul's wisdom in binding the young hero not only into his service but also into his family. Linked by the strongest ties to Jonathan, David also becomes the husband of Michal and thereby the king's son-in-law. The Philistines have been decisively defeated, and David's active role in Israel's army seems designed to insure that this will continue.

Yet again, for the reader—who is by now alert to the fact that the life of Saul rarely runs as smoothly as events first indicate—parallels between this scene and the first encounter with the Philistines (Act I, Scene C) provide misgivings. Once more the initiative lies not in the hands of Saul but of another. This time it is David who sparks the action.[14] Saul, while not actively a hindrance, seems as powerless before the Philistine giant as any other Israelite. He contributes to the event by recognizing the valor of David, once this is demonstrated, and by taking action to insure that this new champion will remain in the forefront of Israel's service. David, like Jonathan before him,[15] initiates the action, and the success is his. On the other hand, parallels in the structure between this encounter and the events narrated in 1 Sam. 11:1–11, 15 serve only to highlight the difference between Saul's role in defense of Jabesh-gilead and in this engagement. In each case a challenge is issued by an alien (11:2; 17:23), sparking terror among the Israelites (11:4; 17:24), leading to a search for a deliverer (11:3–4; 17:25), the appearance of one (11:5–6; 17:25) who succeeds (11:7–11; 17:50) and receives recognition for his actions (11:15; 17:55–58). Then Saul stood forth as hero; now it is David. Then Saul's triumph brought kingship; what must now be in store for David?

Scene C: Saul's failure (1 Sam. 18:6–9a; 19:1–7, 11–17; 26:1–8, 10–14a, 17–22, 25b).   Indeed, the surface stability of II/B soon dissolves and with it Saul's sanity and kingship. His accomplishment of the integration of David into Israel's army and the royal household in II/B is undone by the king himself as he drives David from his court and family into the service of the enemy.[16] In a chiastic reversal of the order in which the relationships were built, David is driven from Jonathan (19:1–7), from Michal (19:11–17), and from Saul himself (26:1–8, 10–14a, 17–22, 25b). The unfortunate impulsiveness that first manifested itself in the opening engagement with the Philistines in ill-timed deeds and oath now manifests itself in jealousy (a jealousy that the reader must ironically note is not really off the mark, given the future course of events). Obsessed with serving his god in 1 Samuel 14, Saul seems now obsessed with the need to destroy David. But the result can only be his own destruction. Once more, while the decision is his, he seems caught up in a nexus of more powerful forces. Seeking to lay hands on David, he only falls into David's hands. Seeking to destroy David, he is spared by his self-made enemy. Events seem beyond his control, and he becomes the subject of mockery. With spear in hand he misses his mark—disintegration is clear. Fate and flaw now work hand in hand to bring down this king who is rejected by the deity, if not by his people.

Act III: Denouement

Scene A: Saul meets Samuel (1 Sam. 28:3–15, 19b–25).   At this point it appears that Saul's end is fixed, and in some respects it is. But all greatness is not to be denied this man of such promising beginnings. He can still command an army in the field against the Philistines, and he can still rely on the personal devotion of loyal followers (28:23; 31:4–6). Moreover, he still commands powers deep within himself. His end, however, is by now determined, and the third encounter with the now dead Samuel simply and bluntly drives this home. The events are fixed; Saul will die. Only the quality of his last days is still his to determine. The facts are there, fixed by dark forces at play throughout his life, but the ability to respond and thereby determine the nature and meaning of his denouement remains. The tragic hero lives within a fixed nexus of forces and events he is powerless to change, but significant choices and patterns of action nevertheless confront him within that prescribed context. It is Saul's decisions and actions in those his last days that finally etch his image as heroic and his life as tragic.

At first glance it might seem that this is not to be the case. The Philistines have rallied against Israel at Mount Gilboa in the north. Saul seems as tied as ever to the deity and his prophet when he once more seeks Samuel. It is an act of desperation, for the normal and the legitimate means of divine-human communication are all silent: "And when Saul inquired of Yahweh, Yahweh did not answer him, either by dreams, or by Urim, or by prophets" (28:6; cf. 14:37). Recourse is had, therefore, to an old woman, a medium in control of a pit in a cave at Endor from which she can summon those in the nether world to communicate with the living. The irony is that this mode of trafficking with the dead was deemed illegitimate in normative Israelite circles, and in fact, Saul, in what must surely have been one more attempt to serve and please the deity, had driven such mediums from the land (28:3). Now he must have the one old woman who escaped his purge sought out, and through her he meets Samuel for a last time. As before, Samuel declares in a private setting what the future holds for Saul: defeat and death with his sons on Mount Gilboa. In Samuel's earlier announcements, there was a note of ambiguity. Saul was to be a leader of his people, but this was announced in the context of strange happenings and in secret. Later on, divine authority is withdrawn from Saul, but he seems to remain king and command the loyalty of many. This final encounter between king and prophet leaves no room for ambiguity: "Tomorrow you and your sons shall be with me" (28:19). Saul sees clearly and fully what must come, and the reader sees as well; perceptions of audience and actor have coincided.

But the nature of Saul's response is still open. When told of his earlier rejection by Yahweh, the king almost pitifully clings to Samuel and whatever support he might wring from him (15:24–31). All self-assertion and willingness to defend his actions quickly dissolve. Now he is faced with the notice of his own death. After a moment's weakness, he takes refreshment at the urging of the old medium and his servants (28:20–25)[17] and then "rose and went away that night" (28:25). The terse quality of the narrative underscores his own resolve. Events are now related in few words, and for the purposes of the narrative few are needed. Saul accepts his fate, marches into it, and thereby makes it his own. In Aristotelian terms, Saul's *anagnorisis,* his recognition scene, takes place in the cave at Endor.[18] Like

Oedipus, he finally comes to see what must be; like Gilgamesh upon his loss of the plant of life, he accepts what has been set for him and knows now where his own deeds necessarily must lead.

Scene B: The death of King Saul (1 Samuel 31). As he moves from the depths of the cave to the top of the mountain, Saul understands and accepts. If the third meeting with Samuel is his *anagnorisis,* his *peripeteia,* the reversal of fortune, comes on Gilboa. Wounded in the last battle that he will fight, he takes his life rather than become an object of scorn and mockery in the hands of the Philistines (he will be no Samson; 31:4–6). A lingering note of irony remains, for Saul is even here not fully in control. His aide refuses the wounded king's last request that he slay him; one might recall an earlier scene in which the will of the king's followers ran counter to his own (14:45; cf. 11:15). Then the people intercede to save Jonathan and salvage the day, leaving the king thwarted and helpless before a course of events that outrun him. Now Jonathan is dead and the battle lost. But the king is not helpless. He falls upon his own sword. By following him in death, his attendant demonstrates that his hesitation was rooted in devotion to his master. (The reader might even recall an earlier scene in which the king's desires were resisted by an aide [1 Sam. 9:5–8]. The young Saul could then accept the advice of his attendant.) In the end, by taking his own life he honors his aide's desires once more. These two episodes bracket the story of the rise and fall of Israel's first king.

This small point of irony in Saul's last moments opens onto a larger irony that informs the act of suicide. On one level this can be seen as the ultimate assertion of human self-control. Death cannot be avoided, but one can determine the time and manner of death. Yet this is also the ultimate act of self-negation. One can make this final assertion of one's control of death only in destroying oneself. Death in battle was Saul's announced fate; indeed, the reader and he now sense that it was the fate to which he was led both by his god and by his own actions from the outset. By acknowledging this fate he makes it his own, he seizes it, not in meek surrender but in the strength of choice. Oedipus's self-blinding act transformed his fate from humble surrender to a heroic fall; Gilgamesh's last hymn to Uruk turned his defeat into mature acceptance. Saul likewise is not passive but acts once more, this time in harmony with forces against which he so often and unintentionally fought.

Outside the brackets provided by the encounters with his aides with which his life as king began and ended are set the formal honors granted the hero of our story. At the outset we encountered a noble and striking young man in an introduction modulated by a faint disquietude. That undercurrent has surfaced in a crescendo. Now it is time for honor once more, this time laced with no ambiguity. The ever grateful men of Jabesh-gilead come and take the desecrated bodies of Saul and his sons from the walls of Bethshan, return with them to Jabesh-gilead, and there cremate them and give them respectful burial. In death Saul receives the honors clearly due him.

THE TRAGEDY OF KING SAUL

This proposed reconstruction of the earliest developed narrative stratum in 1 Samuel that deals with Saul is at points interrupted by material of a different character and thrust. At times this material even dominates the present text. This is the result of a later recasting of the early stratum, recasting that was deemed essential because of its controlling vision. It is the tragic vision that informs this earliest story of Saul.

Of noble birth and heroic stature, Saul is qualified within the classical mode to fill the tragic role. He is an appealing figure when first we meet him, and the potential found in him seems to be realized as his private designation by Yahweh's prophet finds public recognition following his defense of Jabesh-gilead. Yet faint disquietude underlies these early scenes. Samuel speaks for Yahweh and retains this power. Saul's own actions are as much in the spontaneous pattern of the older leaders of the federation in moments of crisis as they are in the still nascent patterns of established kingship. As we have seen, Saul is a man caught in a point of transition between forms of leadership, patterns of politics, and visions of the ways of Yahweh with his people. By the end of Act I, the disquieting undertones have become too apparent to neglect. In the first encounter with the Philistines, Saul's hasty actions in supposed service of his god only serve to blunt the action as the course of events overtake him. And the deity who called him to leadership is for a time silent, speaking again through the lot only to designate Jonathan, the hero of the day and Saul's heir, as the violator of the king's oath. It is the voice of the army and not the voice of Saul or his god that saves Jonathan.

In the opening encounter with Samuel in Act II, we find the prophet and his god now in open opposition to Saul. The reasons for this remain obscure. In spite of attempts by the king to retain their support, he is condemned—ostensibly on a rigid construction of an ancient practice by a harsh Samuel—because he allowed his army to save some livestock from captured booty to sacrifice to the deity (there is no reason to doubt this claim) and because he spared a defeated king.[19] For this reason, divine and prophetic support are withdrawn, and it is Samuel who, on behalf of his god, hacks apart the captured Agag. Saul gave heed to his troops, sought to honor his god, spared a life—and lost a kingdom. The earlier silence of the deity and the terse communication when the silence is broken now underscores a hostility that the king's deeds fail fully to justify. In this context the success of David as he enters the story can only serve further to effect the disintegration of the king. The man who earlier acted with a spontaneity that could be linked with the older "judges" of Israel now goes mad. Saul's every action only accents his fate until, in the face of a final divine silence (28:6), he confronts his destiny and embraces it.

This story is intensely personal. In Saul we have an unrelieved portrait of a great man, confronted with forces beyond his control and comprehension, who is driven into jealousy and then madness. Other characters are also sketched with depth and complexity, and the relationships between them are finely drawn. The triangles formed by Saul, *Jonathan,* and David and then by Saul, *Michal,* and David depict nicely the tensions that emerge in human allegiances and result in unique portraits of the person in the middle. Jonathan and Michal are poignant figures drawn between loyalty to parent and devotion to friend and husband; they are minor figures in a large drama, but finely drawn nevertheless. The most complex of all the relationships is that comprised by Saul, Samuel, and Yahweh. Eager to please deity and prophet, Saul is harshly rebuffed. Anxious to serve, he is strangely alienated from both. His appeals are met with rebuke and silence. Yet it had been the deity and his prophet who called him to deliver Israel, summoned him to a position that was interlaced with the destructive tension that would finally spell doom. Called as leader *(nāgîd)* he has to act and succeed as a king *(melek).* The authority of the latter position is, however, withheld by Samuel in the name of Yahweh. Throughout, Saul's links to deity and prophet remain so strong that even when the only word left is clearly one of utter defeat and death he seeks them out by the only means left.

In all respects, however, Saul is not simply the passive tool of dark forces that would drive him like a bit of wood cast about on the ocean's waves. He accepts the people's designation of him as their *melek.* He believes he can bring Yahweh into his wars. *His* is the ill-timed oath in the first encounter with the Philistines, *his* the sentence of death uttered against his son. *His* is the decision to heed the army and also to spare Agag of the Amalekites, *his* the decision to drive David from him. Throughout he acts and is responsible for his actions. Yet it is difficult to condemn the figure who heeds his army's request to honor his god and who spares the life of an enemy defeated in war. And the reader knows that Saul's fears of David will not prove unfounded. He acts, and his actions are necessary to the outcome of the drama, but they are also caught up in a larger nexus of dimly perceived forces that alone are sufficient to bring about the denouement. Fate and flaw work hand in hand.

There is a hubris in Saul's oath, just as there is in the vow of Oedipus to avenge the prior king's murder and play the role of son to him. Kings must shape and control events and sustain patterns of life. Their subjects turn to them when events threaten death or chaos. They are asked to construct contexts for others to live in, and their comprehension and authority must be adequate to the task. Saul's oath was designed to insure total victory; Oedipus's was to restore plague-stricken Thebes. Yet both men were mortal, and the cosmos larger than their grandest vision. The benefit they sought for their subjects could be obtained only at a terrible price. They had to pay it even if they did not foresee it. The position they are placed in and their self-assurance of their adequacy to meet the challenge, to assess all implications of the situation and to deal with them, drives them to impose their understanding on a reality larger and deeper than they can know. This necessity leads them into deeper errors, as both Saul and Oedipus unjustly accuse one close to them (one linked by marriage) of plotting to take the throne. Saul turns against David; Oedipus unjustly indicts Creon. Neither will heed the moderate advice of cooler minds. From their vantage point reality must conform to the imaginations of their hearts. But it will not do so. They see more than most men, but critical facts remain unseen. Kings must act, and act they do. Fate and flaw work hand in hand. Saul acts to shape a context for life and peace for his people; this is his duty. But he, like Oedipus, fails to recognize that as mortal he is not all-sufficient and that he must act within a nexus of forces beyond his knowledge. Only slowly is their blindness to this removed—at the cost of Oedipus's sight and of Saul's life.

To this is added still another level of irony: both kings accuse another of seeking the throne, another who will in time occupy the throne. Creon comes to succeed Oedipus, as every Greek in Sophocles's audience knew. David, as all Israel knew, was to become king in the place of Saul.

Fate in the tragedy of King Saul is clearly the work of Yahweh. There is no doubt that behind the action stands a deity whose will cannot be thwarted. The authority and power of this deity are not in doubt. This deity's goodness and justice in relation to Saul's intentions and deeds, however, are called into question. We are given in this narrative a depiction of what becomes in essence a savage god. Placing his "chosen" in an impossible position, he drives him to his doom. Yet Saul retains, or rather regains, his stature. In the depths of the cave at Endor and on Gilboa's height, Saul faces the incomprehensible and accepts his fate. In this he moves, in the words of R. B. Sewall, from "a condition of pain and fear, to the condition of suffering—which is the condition of pain and fear contemplated and spiritualized."[20] Pressed to the harsh limits imposed by a savage god, Saul confronts his particular boundary situation in his suicide and receives at last the honor he again merits.

Perhaps the finest response to this tragedy comes in words beyond it, words of one uniquely positioned to respond. When David is informed of Saul's death, he begins to lament: " 'Thy glory, O Israel, is slain upon the high places! How are the mighty fallen!' " (2 Sam. 1:19). In that "How," that mix of exclamation and deep questioning, is found the most adequate response to the tragedy of King Saul.

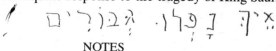

NOTES

1. See D. M. Gunn, *The Fate of King Saul: An Interpretation of a Biblical Story*, JSOTS 14 (Sheffield: JSOT Press, 1980), chap. 1.

2. W. Lee Humphreys, "The Tragedy of King Saul: A Study of the Structure of 1 Samuel 9–31," *JSOT* 6 (1978): 18–27; idem, "The Rise and Fall of King Saul: A Study of an Ancient Narrative Stratum in 1 Samuel," *JSOT* 8 (1980): 74–90; idem, "From Tragic Hero to Villain: A Study of the Figure of Saul and the Development of 1 Samuel," *JSOT* 22 (1982): 95–117.

3. I have found it helpful in teaching 1 Samuel to request three readings of the book, each from the perspective of a different figure: first Saul, then Samuel, then David. It is stunning how the same material will appear in starkly different lights depending on whose perspective and whose questions and values govern the reading of it.

4. An indirect and somewhat different account of Saul's death is found in 2 Sam. 1:1–10. He is on occasion referred to elsewhere in relation to his descendants and those who served him while he lived, in David's lament, and in Nathan's oracle to David (2 Sam. 7:15b). All the Chronicler has to say about Saul is found in 1 Chronicles 10. Verses 1–12 give an account of his

death, and vv. 13–14 offer an indictment of him for "he did not keep the command of Yahweh, and also consulted a medium, seeking guidance." In the light of later developments of the figure of Saul, it is interesting that throughout 1 and 2 Kings rulers of northern Israel are indicted by the Deuteronomistic historian in terms of the archetypal Jeroboam ben Nebat and not Saul ben Kish.

5. Clearly, some links take us even beyond the bounds of 1 Samuel, as the figure of Samuel in 1 Samuel 7 looks back to the major judges, and 2 Samuel 1 picks right up on the events at the close of 1 Samuel and follows the career of David.

6. See Humphreys, "Tragedy of King Saul," 23, for further links.

7. See Humphreys, "Rise and Fall of King Saul."

8. See Humphreys, "From Tragic Hero to Villain," for further development and justification.

9. Note its integration into a full story in Genesis 39, where the notice of Joseph's physical quality is reserved until his encounter with Potiphar's wife (Gen. 39:6b) and becomes a critical theme in the narrative.

10. On this title, see now Baruch Halpern, *The Constitution of the Monarchy in Israel*, HSM 25 (Chico, Calif.: Scholars Press, 1981), chap. 1.

11. Note the fuller basis for this episode provided by the Samuel scroll from Qumran (4QSam[a]; cf. Josephus, *Antiquities* 6.68–71). See P. Kyle McCarter, *1 Samuel*, AB 8 (New York: Doubleday & Co., 1980), 198–99.

12. It will be suggested below that the particular notice of the spirit's rushing upon Saul in 11:6 as well as in 10:6 (cf. 16:13) is the result of prophetic reworking of the older stratum to stress particular concerns of later circles. See below, 52–59.

13. Gunn, *Fate of King Saul*, 41–56.

14. David's links with Jonathan would be developed later by royalist circles to make him a replacement for Jonathan. See below, 59–64.

15. We must remember that the reader of this early stratum would not need 1 Sam. 16:1–13 to know that David would in fact succeed Saul as king, the position that would naturally fall to Jonathan.

16. As noted above, it is quite possible that elements of the early stratum have been at this point replaced by other traditions and are thus lost to us.

17. We should note the sympathetic manner of her depiction throughout the chapter.

18. Aristotle, *Poetics,* chap. 9.

19. No reason is given for this, but we might note that a former enemy now spared could be a valuable asset on Saul's southern flank as he had to continue to face the Philistines. Later Jewish tradition would settle the score between the house of Saul and that of Agag in the defeat by Mordecai (ben Jair, ben Shimei, ben Kish) of Harman (the Agagite) as recounted in the Book of Esther.

20. Sewall, *Vision of Tragedy,* 6.

CHAPTER 3

From Tragic Hero
to Villain

We have already seen that the tragic vision has profound if disquieting theological dimensions, and in the last chapter we considered some of these in what we can now call the "Tragedy of King Saul." Over against the tragic Saul stands a god who seems in many ways savage. The stark quality of this vision of the deity will become all the more apparent as we set this early tragic account of Saul's rise and fall in the particular context in which it seems to have been composed and then trace the ways it was recast by later hands.

TEMPERING AN "ENLIGHTENMENT"

Since G. von Rad's treatment of the period of David and Solomon, biblical scholarship has commonly characterized the united monarchy as an "enlightenment." By this is meant primarily that a break with past traditions, modes of expression, and ways of viewing the world, Yahweh, and humankind had taken place. New visions of the ways of the deity with human beings, new visions of human potential and responsibility, and new forms of literary, religious, and theological expression were created. Beyond this, the term denotes a period of intense excitement, of movement and change that impacted all areas and strata of life. In a context of this sort, some people were stimulated by the changing currents and new possibilities for creative endeavors and experimentation; others found all safe moorings threatened and, afraid of being set adrift in chaotic seas of change, grasped with ever more desperate strength onto whatever of the past still seemed at hand. This reactionary dimension of such profound change—together with its unsettling social, political, and economic transformations that benefited some at the expense of others—must temper some of the more heady connotations of the term "enlightenment." In fact, criticism of the term's applicability to Solomon's reign has been voiced recently.[1] As even the old Deuteronomistic tradition itself makes clear—and most recent histories of ancient Israel follow it—all was not brightness under Kings David and Solomon. Yet the attribution to that period of such literary units as the so-called Succession Narrative of 2 Samuel 9—20, 1 Kings 1—2, the Joseph story of Genesis 37, 39—48, 50, and the Yahwist's theological-historical epic narrative of Israel's origins and mission, as well as certain basic wisdom traditions, remains plausible. Indeed, even these products of this "enlightenment," which recognize in their own ways new levels of human potential, also contain strong warning about the possibility of their abuse and hint at dark judgments that must then follow. However, even darker possibilities are most forcibly presented, I have argued, in another unit that I would attribute to this period: "The Tragedy of King Saul."

I have given reasons elsewhere for the placing of the composition of the tragedy of King Saul in the context of the united monarchy, and a brief summary will suffice here.[2] The material outlined in the last chapter that constitutes the tragedy of King Saul imparts the overarching structure to 1 Samuel 9—31. Yet as it now stands, that structure is at points broken as attention turns to other figures and concerns, and the finely articulated narrative pattern is interrupted by material dealing solely with Samuel (1 Samuel 12) or with David (1 Samuel 21–22; 23; 27:1—28:2; 29—30). The simplest explanation for this is that an early narrative centered on Saul was later supplemented, expanded, and thereby recast by other hands, providing many of the tensions and ambiguities that characterize the perspectives on the figure of Saul in 1 Samuel 9—31 as we now have it. Saul and his rise and fall were the concerns of the early stratum. In later recastings of it he came to be overshadowed first by Samuel and then by David, and the tight pattern of the older story was fractured at points, even if it is still apparent in 1 Samuel 9—31. Thus, the stratum designated the tragedy of King Saul must be early.

Beyond this we should note that a range of motifs within this material, and distinct characteristics of it, set it apart from most Hebraic narrative. Especially in the denouement, we find a set of practices that seem distinctly non-Israelite. Saul's quest for information about the future through consultation with a ghost is one outstanding example; elsewhere, this is roundly condemned in Israelite tradition (Lev. 19:31; 20:6, 27; Deut. 18:10–11; 2 Kings 21:6 = 2 Chron. 33:6; 2 Kings 23:24; Isa. 8:19; 29:4) as a parade example of pagan wrongheadedness. And only here in the Hebrew Bible is a dead person denoted as an *'elōhîm,* the regular term for the deity in early Hebraic material. Implied in this is a vision of the dead as more vital—more alive, if you will—than is normal in Hebraic tradition until near the onset of the common era. In this story the dead Samuel can speak with Saul; Saul can be discomforted by him and cause Samuel profound unease in turn. The use of an old woman to call up the dead through a pit in the earth (the basic meaning of the Hebrew term *'ôb*), thereby showing that she is a *ba'alat-'ôb* (mistress of such a pit), is unique in the material found in the Hebrew Bible. Further, we must note that not only is she successful in her attempt, but she is presented in a quite sympathetic manner. At first she is understandably terrified when she recognizes Saul (who has rid the land of her kind), but later she appears as one of the few who remains genuinely concerned for his well-being. In all of this, the most ready and illuminating parallels from the ancient world are found in early Greek and Hittite tradition.[3]

All this suggests that the author of the tragedy of King Saul was one who drew upon perspectives and values rooted in the cultural sphere of the Aegean and of Anatolia as much or more than in Hebraic earth. We know that it was in the courts of David and Solomon that broad contact on many levels with distant parts of the ancient world was fostered. Hittite and Greek roots seem likely for some personalities in their establishments, and among them quite possibly stood the author of "The Tragedy of King Saul."[4] In fact, the very tragic thrust of his narrative is another pointer in the same direction; for as we will now come to see, more normative Hebrew tradition, for all its expansiveness in this period and later, proved to be thin soil indeed for the tragic vision to set its roots. Arguments of this sort are necessarily circumstantial and even circular; yet they can claim a cumulative force of evidence and are all we have. When set in the context of the "enlightenment" of David and Solomon, "The Tragedy of King Saul" appears as a distinctly disquieting contribution to a period of remarkable literary and theological experimentation.

A recent study of the ethos of the united monarchy, with special emphasis on David, is entitled *In Man We Trust.*[5] This title captures the new humanism of this period but is in no way designed to deny a profound vision of Yahweh's role in human affairs as well. A brief review of several items ascribed to this period will define the cultural and theological world into which the tragedy of King Saul was thrust.

The Succession Narrative
(2 Samuel 9—20; 1 Kings 1—2)[6]

This remarkable account of the latter part of David's reign, with its concentration on personal and political tensions surrounding the royal family, climaxing in the ascension of Solomon to the throne, has been hailed as a master work of Israelite historiography and narrative art. Von Rad in particular has called attention to the new and subtle (some would say, more mature) view of divine providence that pervades the work. Essentially, the story is set on the human plane. Action is initiated for good or ill by human beings, and they and others feel the impact of this action, often for years to come. The crass "taking" of a man's wife and the murder of this man, who is an alien (a Hittite), by a despotic David brings a curse on him and his house that rolls on through the years. The royal family seems self-destructive, as a son rapes his half-sister, her brother murders the rapist, father and son are alienated and then uneasily reunited, only to be finally separated in an attempted coup. The narrative ends with a final struggle to seize the throne of the aged David, a struggle in which Solomon is thoroughly if brutally triumphant, taking the throne into hands stained with the blood of many. Real figures, drawn in forceful if often muted shades, populate the narrative. Feelings that are humanly understandable too often lead to actions that we cannot condone. One crass human deed sets a whole chain of violent actions in motion.

Through it all, Yahweh seems strangely absent. This, however, is just an impression gained from a reading of the surface of the story. It is essentially about human deeds and their consequences, human decisions and responsibility for them. Only twice, as von Rad points out, is a programmatic statement about Yahweh made by the narrator (2 Sam. 12:24–25; 17:14). While this may overstate the case (see, e.g., 11:26; 12:15), the difference between this and earlier Israelite material—in which Yahweh is so often dramatically active as the decisive force in human affairs, often breaking in with miracles—is striking. No regular, direct, divine-human dialogue is found here: no splitting of seas, no manna or fire from heaven, no thunder and hail on enemy forces, no opening of the earth to swallow up evil men and women in this narrative. Yet these brief programmatic notices stress that behind the human initiatives, for which the humans are responsible, a broader divine purpose will be realized. At least in terms of David and his dynasty, this purpose is ultimately for human good. A family that seemed determined to self-destruct is preserved on the throne in Jerusalem, and the dynasty is secure. Not that all suffering is done away with in an instant, nor that humans do not reap what they sow in violence and discord, but through and in spite of it all, the divine will for good will not be defeated. This vision of providence working out in good for human protagonists does not annul human freedom and the responsibility that goes with it. In fact, this narrative seems to stress human potential—for good or ill—in ways not present in earlier literature. There is an ambiguous note at the end: David's act of self-serving violence wreaks havoc in his family; blood shed in securing his throne stains Solomon's hands. He is the beloved of Yahweh who will be called Yahweh's son as well (2 Sam. 7:12–14); yet so was David. Yahweh's loving support is secure, but it will not annul royal freedom to act nor the responsibility for these actions.

The Joseph Story
(Genesis 37, 39—48, 50)[7]

Broadly speaking, the Joseph story is cut from the same cloth: we encounter the same vision holding in balance a benevolent providence and human freedom; we meet another family bent on self-destruction. A spoiled youngest son doted upon by a blind father, jealous older brothers, boasting about dreams, violence, deceit: of such is the story of Jacob's family composed. Again, characters are cast in mixed and muted tones, in which sympathy must be mixed with disapproval. Jacob's excessive fondness for the only son of a most loved wife is human and understandable, but its expression without regard to the consequence or feelings of his other sons cannot be condoned; the brothers' feelings strike a sympathetic cord but their deeds repel. In time, as Joseph is transformed and able to take revenge, we may understand, but part of us must draw back as he causes his brothers to suffer years of torment and allows his father to continue to grieve over him. Only after years of agony and fear are reconciliation, forgiveness, and reunion finally attained—but not before each figure in his own way has reaped the fruits of his actions. Each character is profoundly changed in the course of the story as well.

Once again, the deity seems to be in the background of the narrative for the most part. Yahweh appears not as a sudden and dramatic force but as a dimly perceived thrust toward ultimate life and blessing in a situation interlaced with violence, deceit, and curse. Once again, it is von Rad who makes this clear in his discussion of the two statements by Joseph, in which the benevolent care of Yahweh is underscored.[8] When he first reveals his identity to his brothers, Joseph hastens to reassure them in their stunned silence: " 'God sent me before you to preserve for you a remnant on earth, and to keep alive for you many survivors' " (Gen. 45:7). After the death of their father, he again reassures them:

> "Fear not, for am I in the place of God? As for you, you meant evil against me; but God meant it for good, to bring it about that many people should be kept alive, as they are today." (Gen. 50:19–20)

Joseph's words capture the two-edged quality of the situation nicely. "You meant evil" (he might have said "we"), and evil was the result of their actions, for others and for themselves. "But God meant it for good"; in spite of all they did, the family was reunited, preserved intact, and sustained. Human deeds are played out and caught up in a larger, divinely determined nexus that is benevolent, that creates and sustains life, even as it allows full play to human freedom. Once again, beneficent providence and human freedom and responsibility are held in balance.

The Yahwist's Epic[9]

We cannot begin here to treat this vast and many-faceted narrative of the world's and Israel's origins (called J by biblical scholars). In its own way, and with varied results for the wide range of traditions gathered and ordered by the Yahwist, the same general themes are affirmed that we found informing the succession narrative and the Joseph story. A peaceable kingdom created by the deity is shattered through human disobedience (Genesis 2—3).[10] In spite of repeated attempts by the deity to stem the resulting flow of curse, the course of human history leads to ever more violent dissolution of the created ideal (Genesis 4, 6—9, 11). Finally, with nations scattered and unable to communicate due to a thwarted attempt to scale the heavens and make a name, the deity elects one from among these nations to be his special people and restore harmony and blessing to all (Gen. 12:1–3). So begins a story that will climax in the establishment of Israel in southern Palestine and by implication in the kingdom ruled by the Davidic house.

Here again we note the dual theme. On the one hand, human beings can act for good or ill. On the other, the deity acts for blessing and life both on behalf of his chosen and through them for all humankind. His support for the chosen nation is unqualified. Genesis

12:10–20 sets forth this dual perspective nicely and stands as an epitome of the outlook of the Yahwist. Abraham is free to leave the land of promise on his own initiative, free to lie about his relationship with Sarah. And his actions bring dire results in a plague on Egypt— he is hardly a force for blessing upon that land! When he is found out by Pharaoh and expelled, his plans seem about to come to nothing. Yet Pharaoh does not act as Abraham seemed sure he would—he does not slay Abraham and simply take Sarah (even after Abraham's lie offered some further provocation).[11] Abraham is expelled, but the note at the end of the episode tells us he leaves with all he had gained while in Egypt (quite likely as a bride price for Sarah) along with the wife he brought with him. Embarassed, perhaps, he nevertheless comes off quite well. Chastened for his deeds, he is nevertheless upheld; endangered by his actions, he is preserved. His very human actions make a difference, but they are also caught up in a larger nexus designed to secure blessing above and beyond the immediate outcome of human intentions and deeds.

Early Wisdom Literature

The three items discussed above reveal at once the variety within the literary repertoire of the united monarchy and certain uniform underlying perspectives on the ways of the deity with human beings and especially with his elect. Wisdom materials like those found in Proverbs 10—30, which tradition assigns in part to Solomon's sponsorship, develop the same broad perspective.[12] Simply to summarize, the sayings in Proverbs are designed for human assessment, testing, and application. They assign to human intent and action high significance and responsibility and in this regard can be regarded as quite humanistic. We must make decisions, we can make informed decisions, and we must bear responsibility for their results. Yet this is again the case within a larger frame of meaning that is the work of the deity. The following observations that characterize wisdom's perspectives provide an overview of this: (a) The world in which we live and act is a cosmos; it is ordered. It is not chaos or the result of pure chance. Certain types of action will bring certain results. (b) This design is the work of its creator/sustainer who is Yahweh. (c) To a significant degree the orders and patterns that define creation as cosmos and not chaos are knowable and teachable. To this end the material in the collections in Proverbs is designed. This does not, however, deny any element of the mysterious or of divine freedom (Prov. 16:1, 2, 9; 20:30, 31, for example); creation does not define or limit the creator. (d) Even elements of the mysterious can be readily accepted within the certainty that the creator and therefore the creation are ultimately beneficent, that justice, blessing, goodness, and life hold at the center of the cosmos. Divine goodness can be affirmed even when not apparent for a time. It is only at the end of decades that Joseph, for example, can make the affirmations we cited above, but he can make them with confidence for all that. There is enough to allow the empirical eye to sustain the eye of faith.

It is in this context that the tragedy of King Saul strikes so disquieting a note. The tragic vision in its own way must also affirm the first two statements just made. It will agree that human actions are significant and that one bears a level of responsibility for what one does. This is caught up in a larger context defined by the deity. However it may appear to the contrary at times—and one thinks of Saul in his desperate attempt to harness events in 1 Samuel 14—we inhabit a cosmos and not chaos. Moreover, tragedy would affirm that this is the work of the deity. But it is at this point that the challenge comes. In the face of the tragedy of King Saul, who could dare assert that the divine will is comprehensible to a significant degree, or especially that it is ultimately good? The elements of divine mystery and freedom loom not only large but ominous. They can strike at the very heart of the life of some human beings as a destructive and savage force, turning well-intended designs into havoc and calling forth the darkest forces out of a great man's psychic depths. The savage god may have his ways and designs, but they can appear genuinely arbitrary to mortals and terrifyingly destructive to some. No one stands at the end of 1 Samuel 31 in the role of Joseph to affirm that "God meant it for good." Joseph, his brothers, and Jacob are in the end united once more in Egypt, where they will find their lives preserved in the face of both famine and their own destructive designs of the past. They have suffered and in suffering gained a perspective that changes them. This change allows, within the providence of their god, renewed life. Death comes only in old age, with full measure of dignity and peace. Saul is united with his sons but only as they fall in life's prime, in battle on Mount Gilboa. Saul's recognition, the perspective he gains through his suffering and especially in his final encounter with Samuel in the cave at Endor, can lead only to his and Israel's defeat in battle and to suicide. Here David's words of lament are a more fitting epitaph, words that are circumspectly silent about the place of the deity in these events. It is as if, beyond their deeds and in a strange way through them, Joseph and his family are finally fated for reconciliation and new life by a benevolent deity. Saul seems fated as well, as we have suggested, but his fate is dark indeed. In the case of the family of the patriarch, human flaw and divine design work together to renew life and reconcile the alienated; blessing comes from curse. In the case of Saul, flaw and fate work only to destroy.

Perhaps it can be said of Saul that he, too, meant it for evil; his final pursuit of David might qualify. But generally his deeds are more ambiguous. His deeds are necessary for his fall, but they are not sufficient to account for it. This comes into stark focus when an encounter between king and prophet in the tragedy of King Saul is set in parallel with a similar encounter between king and prophet in the Succession Narrative. In 1 Samuel 15, Saul is commanded by Samuel in Yahweh's name to undertake an action. This he does and in his own eyes fulfills his charge. In 2 Samuel 12, David is depicted as undertaking an action without thought of Yahweh; in the end, it brings Uriah to an early grave and the widowed Bathsheba to his bed. Each king is rebuked by a prophet in the name of Yahweh for what he did. Saul spared a defeated king and preserved some booty to offer to the deity; David is indicted for fundamental disregard of human life. Each man acknowledges his guilt. In response to David, Nathan said, "Yahweh also has put away your sin; you shall not die" (2 Sam. 12:13). Saul, on the other hand, is set on a course that will lead through madness to Gilboa, and no relenting word is heard. It is true that a pattern of violence is set in motion through David's family that causes him deep suffering. But his life and his dynasty are preserved; his heir will, in fact, come from his union with Bathsheba. Jonathan, Saul's heir, dies in his father's last battle. It is true that Samuel does turn back after Saul and that Saul worships Yahweh (1 Sam. 15:31), but only after Saul's fate has been fixed.

In each of the literary units assigned to Israel's united monarchy, there is a coherence. This coherence is provided by the will of Yahweh. It is revealed, for example, in the brief notice about the deity's love for the second child of David and Bathsheba who comes in time to secure the throne and dynasty (2 Sam. 12:24–25). It is found in the initial dreams of Joseph which point to a pattern of events that do, in fact, work out as determined (Gen. 42:9; 50:18). It is there in the promise and mission set forth for Abraham and his seed in the Yahwist's epic (Gen. 12:1–3). In all of this there is also an element of the arbitrary: in the love of the deity for Solomon, in the support of a young and spoiled Joseph, even in the choice of Abraham. There is coherence in the tragedy of King Saul as well. Things do not happen by chance. But in this case all comes together—not in a family reunited, a dynasty and throne secure, a promise fulfilled, but in a family destroyed, a dynasty aborted, a throne lost, great promises unrealized, and in a death by suicide of one who recognizes that this is the only human act left to him. In this we, as well as those first caught up in the excitement of Israel's golden age, glimpse something of the dark side of the attempt to define the proper mix of human potential and the ways of the god who shapes this cosmos. For a moment the secret terrors of the human condition, rooted in the ancient myths and legends now recast or rejected by the new spirit of enlightenment, resurface with a force not to be denied. Against this experience of the savage god and the vital flaw in the greatest of human potential, all other assertions about divine benevolence, justice of the cosmos, and unlimited human capability must be tested and refined. In this the tragedy of King Saul stands as a tempering challenge to an "enlightenment" that many would later look back on as Israel's golden age. It certainly stands as a distinct contribution to what was, by all accounts, a time of literary and theological excitement and creativity that has informed, as few eras have, the traditions of the Western world.

A PROPHETIC PERSPECTIVE
ON KING SAUL

The evolution of 1 Samuel is complex. We have already suggested that undergirding chapters 9—31 is an old narrative unit we have referred to as "The Tragedy of King Saul." This itself was composed, in the period of the united monarchy, of a range of once distinct units, each with its own prior history. This early narrative stratum is now embedded in 1 Samuel, having been recast and added to substantially. Even though its structure still informs 1 Samuel 9—31, substantial changes were made in the early stratum, and its tragic perspective was fundamentally skewed. We do not here intend to give a full history of the development of 1 Samuel—were that possible—but rather to note two important stages that are of special interest to us in this study because they reveal ways in which later Israelite circles dealt with a tragic vision that they found antithetical to all they wished to affirm about Yahweh. The tragic vision stands as a basic counterpoint to essential elements of the Hebraic religious tradition, and these are highlighted as these circles attempt to deal with it.

As 1 Samuel now stands, the reader does not meet Saul until almost a third of the way through, for only after an extended intro-

duction to the figure of Samuel[13] is the young man Saul brought onto
the stage. The effect of this is to place him in the shadow of Samuel, a
shadow that continues to dominate his life until its end. Not only does
the figure of Samuel precede Saul on the stage, but linked with him is
Israel's request for a king and an evaluation of that request that sets a
distinct perspective from which the story of Saul is now to be read.
That perspective is reinforced by additions made to Saul's own story
as it unfolds. The tragedy of King Saul becomes part of a larger
drama involving the establishment of kingship in Israel and the integration of this political transition into Israel's theological traditions.

Thus, the reader is first introduced to Samuel through his remarkable birth narrative: this child, who was a special gift of the deity to
his barren mother and then her gift in return to her god (1 Samuel
1),[14] is clearly no ordinary mortal. The account of his early years of
service in the temple at Shiloh, interlaced with material dealing with
the rejection of the priestly house of Eli, serve further to reinforce
this (3:1—4:1). Of particular importance here is the fact that Samuel
is marked as the one through whom Yahweh speaks, at a time when
divine words and vision were rare (1 Sam. 3:1). In his audition in the
temple at night before the ark, his prophetic credentials are firmly
established:

> And Samuel grew, and Yahweh was with him and let none of his words
> fall to the ground. And all Israel from Dan to Beer-sheba knew that
> Samuel was established as a prophet of Yahweh. (1 Sam. 3:19–20)

He is next encountered in 1 Samuel 7 as judge and war leader, placing
him firmly in the traditions of the federation (see, e.g., Deborah and
Jephthah). Among other things, this unit (7:5–12, 16–17)[15] serves to
preclude use of the Philistine threat to Israel to legitimize any demand for a king. When Yahweh is fully recognized by Israel as its
warrior and sovereign (7:8), he is more than able and willing to
protect his own; human initiative is kept to a bare minimum (7:10–
11).[16] Then, when the request for a king is forthcoming anyway, the
opportunity is provided to set out a distinct and limiting perspective
on kingship. B. Birch has aptly characterized this as the "sinful-but-
still-of-God" view of kingship.[17] Only with reluctance do the deity and
his prophet allow a king, and it is stressed that human kingship is in
no way to compromise the sovereignty of Yahweh (8:7) and, by
implication, those who speak directly for him. It is clear that the
perspective here offered is broadly prophetic, stemming from a circle

that found its ideological roots in the figure of Samuel, the most forceful representative of their point of view, at least until Elijah.

This perspective is established upon a particular frame of reference, a distinct mode of understanding Yahweh and the Israelite's relationship with him. The roots of this are set deep in the traditions of the federation and need not be traced here in detail. As sovereign, Yahweh commands allegiance from his people (subjects) and in return protects them from external danger by fighting their wars and from internal strife by establishing a pattern for law and order. As is made clear in 1 Sam. 8:7, Yahweh is a warrior-king. Human instruments will be used by him as he empowers them, generally for only a period of limited duration, and he will designate some of his people as his prophetic spokesmen. Thus, in 1 Samuel 7 it is Yahweh who routs the Philistines, with Israel involved in only the mopping-up operations. Even Samuel plays no role in the battle itself, his task being to bring the erring subjects back into fidelity with their sovereign deity and to insure a right interpretation of the course of events. The land is Yahweh's, granted by him to Israel for their use as his tenants. Israel's existence as a nation is the work of Yahweh; Israel is his creation, molded from a band of fugitive slaves whom he delivered from Egyptian bondage in what became the archetypal action of the warrior-king in his people's behalf (Exodus 15). It would serve as the model for understanding all later battles fought by him and, relived in regular cultic cycles, as the basis for Israelite allegiance to Yahweh. From this perspective, Yahweh may appear sometimes severe in his demands and uncompromising in his expectations, but he is essentially just. Moreover, it is important to recognize that those demands were articulated to the people through the voice of Yahweh's prophet. Deliverance and nationhood lead to (re-)affirmation of allegiance to the sovereign deity, an allegiance defined by stipulations agreed to freely and in gratitude (Joshua 24). Continued obedience meant sure support and life; disobedience brought harsh but just punishment and the threat of rejection. While full articulation of this perspective came only with the fully developed Deuteronomistic history, its essential roots must be very old and must have informed the understanding of the relationship between deity and people in the federation.

Only after the reader is firmly placed within this perspective in 1 Samuel is Saul introduced. In taking up the tragedy of King Saul at this point, the prophetic circle did not leave it untouched. It has been suggested that even in the opening scene of Act I, their hand is to be seen in 1 Samuel 9:15–17, 20–21; the extended form of 10:1 found in the LXX; and in 10:5–6, 8, 10–13.[18] The effect of this material is to stress the initiative of Yahweh in the selection of Israel's first king and the essential part played by the prophet Samuel. We are introduced as well to the governing role of the spirit of the deity in the transformation of this lad into a ruler, a theme that will also be forcefully developed later. In this way, a partial recentering of the older material has taken place: an old account with strong folkloric characteristics, telling of the young Saul's search for lost asses only to stumble on a kingdom, is now made to stress the formative role of prophet and deity in a basic transformation in Israel's constitution. This is then reinforced in 1 Sam. 10:17–26. By taking the public initiative in the designation of Saul as king through the lot, Yahweh and his prophet are shown to be transforming a situation that would normally call for judgment into an act of grace. A request inviting rebuke is nevertheless granted by the deity.[19] In the process, however, the perspective expressed in 1 Sam. 8:7 is pointedly reinforced (1 Sam. 10:17–19). And it is boldly implied that Yahweh's choice far outstrips any selection that the people may have made on their own (10:24). The fact that in the tragedy of King Saul the first encounter with Samuel and the announcement of Saul's future kingship was a private matter (9:27; 10:14–16) permits the addition of this episode of the prophetic public selection of the king.

The defense of Jabesh-gilead, taken from the older tragic narrative, is now utilized—with minor adjustments—to illustrate the wisdom of Yahweh's selection. While others seem helpless and can only raise a tearful cry, Saul is able through the empowering of Yahweh's spirit (11:6a) to deliver the beleaguered city. The addition of v. 11:6a takes up a prophet's thread from before and serves to reinforce again the active role of the spirit in this king's success (cf. 10:6, 10). The insertion of the phrase "and [after] Samuel" in v. 11:7 brings Yahweh's prophet securely onto the stage. While playing no role in the actual conflict, Samuel is made the instigator of what now becomes, in the light of 1 Sam. 10:17–27, a public renewal of what he and his god have already accomplished (11:14).

Then comes the break between prophet (and deity) and king. In what has been suggested as a prophetic addition to the older stratum in 1 Sam. 10:8, prophetic authority over the actions of kings is stressed. At first glance, Samuel's instructions to Saul seem clear: wait seven days at Gilgal for the prophet, who will offer sacrifices and then tell the king what he is to do. We must note that this verse follows immediately upon, and thereby effectively annuls, the preceding and older notice (10:7b) that the king is to do whatever he feels appropriate ("whatever your hand finds to do"), in the confidence that his god is with him. Soon enough Saul will have little basis for that confidence, finding, indeed, that Yahweh is present only when the prophet is as well and even then that Yahweh is not clearly with him. A first hint of uncertainty is struck when we find Saul's kingship renewed at Gilgal (11:14–15) in the course of which sacrifices are offered: they are not said to be offered by Samuel. Prophetic additions to material from the older stratum thus serve to complicate our perception of Saul's position. Then, in a unit widely recognized as inserted into chapter 13 (vv. 7b-15a), the instructions of 1 Sam. 10:8 are clearly taken up, but uncertainty remains. Samuel is late! Seven days have passed, and Saul's troops are defecting in the face of the Philistine mobilization. Saul takes the initiative and offers sacrifices in preparation for battle. At that point Samuel appears and, without regard for the intent of Saul's action, sharply rebukes him in the name of his god and announces that as a result his dynasty is not to be established. It would appear on first reading that Samuel is in the wrong, and certainly some sympathy is permitted Saul in this, for he has, it seems, at least technically met the requirements set by Samuel. Yet, as D. M. Gunn has demonstrated, 1 Sam. 10:8 is more ambiguous than it first appears: it is possible to read Samuel's instructions in a manner that places less stress on the precise number of days and more on the command to wait for him.[20] This latter is clearly how Samuel decides to read the situation. One may sympathize with Saul, but one must also sense that, in the context of the prophetic recasting of the older stratum, larger issues confront us than the fate of one man. Lines of authority and levels of power are at issue. The relationship between prophet and king especially is at stake, and in this respect the very ambiguity of the charge and varying interpretations of it permit a vivid demonstration of just whose voice will carry the day. Prophets demand obedience, not sympathy. The prophetic addition to the older tragedy also heightens the irony in the remaining events in this episode. Saul's dynasty is not to be established by Yahweh, but all the same it is Jonathan, Saul's natural heir, who is the leader in the subsequent encounter with the Philistines.

We have seen that in the encounter narrated in 1 Samuel 14 Saul's actions serve only to retard the pace of events and blunt Israel's victory (cf. 1 Samuel 7). On the surface, he acts with all the spontaneity of his encounter with the band of prophets in 1 Sam. 10:10 and upon his hearing of the threat to Jabesh-gilead in 1 Sam. 11:4.

After these earlier notices about the role of the spirit, added by prophetic circles, its absence in 1 Samuel 14 should not be over-looked.

The partial break between king and prophet becomes total in the aftermath of Saul's war against the Amalekites. Again, Gunn has demonstrated the ambiguity of the situation, and we have discussed this above.[21] We also suggested that 1 Samuel 15 is throughout heavily recast by prophetic hands, so much so that disentangling the earlier and later material is not possible. This encounter between prophet and king is critical for the prophetic perspective, for now Saul himself is rejected as king by Samuel in the name of his god. Earlier, it was his dynasty that was to fail to continue. This time, relying upon a strict interpretation of Samuel's instructions to the king, Saul is charged with failure to obey (15:22). He is guilty and is rejected. In prophetic eyes absolute obedience to the sovereign Yahweh is demanded of every Israelite in all circumstances—the king is no exception. It is full obedience to every word of Yahweh delivered through the prophet that is required; gradations of disobedience and extenuating circum-stances are not recognized. Motive is irrelevant. The facts on their face accuse Saul, and his excuses are of no avail. The tragic hero of the older stratum now stands in prophetic eyes as an out-and-out villain.

What was announced in 1 Sam. 15:28 is quickly brought to pass by Samuel in 16:1–13. This prophetic unit stands in nice parallel to 10:17–27, as once more prophetic authority in making and breaking kings is forcefully asserted. In fact, Samuel's reluctant obedience when charged with his task by his god (16:15) stands in counterpoint to Saul's presumed disobedience in 1 Samuel 15. As earlier, the new king is empowered by the spirit of Yahweh (16:13, cf. 10:6, 10; 11:6), and in this (the only instance in this material of a clear linkage of David with the spirit of Yahweh) an important subtheme of the prophetic perspective is developed. The evil spirit from the deity then marks the reversal of Yahweh's earlier empowering of Saul (16:14; 18:10–11; 19:8–10, cf. 11:6), as well as setting the stage for one of David's entrances into the court and family of Saul. The remarkable little unit in 1 Sam. 19:18–20 drives this prophetic emphasis home. For one final time the spirit masters Saul, in this case to defeat his evil designs on David and Samuel. On the divine level, power has shifted, and the contrast between this episode and 1 Sam. 10:10 is under-scored by the use of the same adage in each (10:11; 19:24), forming an inclusion around the major portion of Saul's reign. 1 Samuel 10:11

comes just before Saul becomes king, 1 Sam. 19:24 just before his final descent into madness. The spirit that led him into kingship and through his early triumph now drives him out again.

If S. De Vries's analysis of 1 Sam. 17:1—18:2 is correct,[22] a prophetic alternative to the encounter between David and the Philistine giant is preserved as well. He suggests that 1 Sam. 17:1–11, 32–40, 42–48a, 49, 51–54, which alone is preserved in the LXX, represents a coherent and distinct version of this event in which stress is placed on Yahweh's victory over the haughty Philistine. In this version, the uncircumcised challenges Yahweh's sovereignty, a basic concern of the prophetic material throughout, and the insult is met by the deity through his selected human instrument. The text of the LXX indicates that in some circles this form of the tradition stood alone, while the MT is indication that in other circles this form was combined with the older version found in the tragedy of King Saul.[23] As noted above, this older version balanced David's heroic actions on Saul's and Israel's behalf with Saul's wisdom in binding David to his service. This stands in sharp contrast to the prophetic stress on Yahweh's power to defend his good name and people (cf. 1 Samuel 7). Even when the two are combined, as in the MT, the latter perspective seems to prevail.

One last trace of the prophetic hand can be seen in an expansion of Samuel's last terse announcement of Saul's fate in the cave at Endor (28:16–19a). This includes a reference back to the critical chapter 15. Samuel's last indictment makes the situation clear:

> "Yahweh has done to you as he spoke by me; for Yahweh has torn the kingdom out of your hand, and given it to your neighbor, David. Because you did not obey Yahweh, and act upon his burning anger against Amalek, therefore Yahweh has done this thing to you this day." (1 Sam. 28:17–18, RSV revised)

1 Samuel 15 as a whole, especially 15:28, is recalled: "Yahweh has torn the kingdom of Israel from you this day, and has given it to your neighbor, who is better than you." In this matter the prophetic indictment of the disobedient Saul stands uncompromisingly as the basis of the fate that befell him. In prophetic eyes, Saul's death at his own hand was, no doubt, just what one would expect from such a man. The desperate, rejected king who set his will over against that of his god is driven to take his life, a deed unthinkable to most Israelites. One's perspective on a suicide is determined in part by one's vantage point on the life that leads up to it. From the vantage point of the prophet, Saul's was the life of a villain, a man who even as Yahweh's

chosen king turned from his duty of absolute obedience to his sovereign god.

Building on the work of Birch and De Vries, I have argued[24] that this prophetic recasting of the older tragedy of King Saul is to be dated to about the middle of the eighth century B.C.E.—that is, not many years before the fall of Samaria to the army of Assyria. This work represents the end of a process that would have begun much earlier in prophetic circles, even as early as the days of Elijah and Elisha, in which traditions about Samuel were preserved and shaped and finally integrated into the older tragedy of King Saul. In this way the prophetic perspective on kingship in Israel and its relation to Yahweh's sovereignty found legitimization, as the older tragic hero was transformed into a villain, and the savage god of the tragic vision became the severe but just king of Israel. A vision of the deity as firm in his demands and steadfast in his actions in Israel's behalf when obedience is forthcoming controls the prophetic perspective. This vision demanded a new perspective on Israel's fallen first king. This the prophetic hand accomplished in what became an important stage in the development of 1 Samuel. In this the tragic vision was skewed, as the story became one of the determined working out of covenant justice, of the fitting fall of a disobedient king accomplished by a deity who was clearly justified. Indeed, in the older stratum the prophetic circle found material that, when "properly" used and presented, would nicely illustrate their perspective. We have already stressed that the tragic vision must hold fate and flaw in delicate balance. By focusing the reader from the outset on Samuel and his perspective on the deity and king, and through deft additions to the older narrative, this balance is tipped in the direction of flaw and of just divine retribution at the hands of Israel's god and his prophetic spokesmen. More sinner than sinned against, the tragic hero became a villain.

A ROYALIST PERSPECTIVE
ON KING SAUL

The material that would come to comprise our 1 Samuel was to receive further reshaping, and another body of traditions would be woven into it as well. This would reflect a Judean and specifically Davidic perspective, that characteristic of royalist circles active during the reign of Hezekiah. By 722 B.C.E., the northern kingdom of Israel was no more. Fugitives from the final Assyrian assault upon this small state and its capital, Samaria, would have come in some numbers to the state of Judah, the only remaining Israelite vestige of the once impressive empire of David and Solomon. Here they came again under the rule of the Davidic house, from which the northern Israelites had broken two centuries earlier. Now all Israel was potentially united once more under one ruler, and a Davidite at that. Some pretensions toward a return to the golden days of the united monarchy seem to have guided the religious and political policies of Hezekiah.[25] Traditions of northern origin were brought with the fugitives from Samaria—for example, Elohistic traditions (E) on Israel's origins, an early form of the law code standing at the heart of Deuteronomy, the remembered oracles of Amos and Hosea, and a range of prophetic legends and other narratives—and in some cases, these were integrated into Judean materials (E was woven into J) or given a Judean stamp (see Amos 9:11–15; Hosea 2:1–2; 14:9).

Among these materials, it is suggested, was the prophetic corpus dealing with Samuel and Saul that we have considered above. Now in royalist hands, it would provide the basis for the development of an extended account of the origins of kingship in Israel that would climax in the recognition by all of David as Yahweh's chosen. This was accomplished by weaving into the prophetic recasting of the tragedy of King Saul an already developed cycle of material dealing with the rise of David to the throne. As we shall see, the legitimization of Davidic claims to divine election are in this manner demonstrated in striking contrast to the failure and rejection of the house of Saul, Israel's first king. A forceful appeal to northern as well as southern sympathies was made in this, and an explanation is given about why it is that the line of Israel's first king does not still rule. One more critical phase in the development of 1 Samuel is before us, one in which the tragic figure of Saul and the associated image of the deity are again nuanced in a distinct manner. The tragic hero who became a villain is now made to appear as a man cursed and rejected. The once savage god, having been recast into a just sovereign, becomes now the loving father of Davidic kings, giving his unqualified support to them (even if it is tempered at points by discipline and a hint of the arbitrary in his treatment of others).

Judean royalists could accept much in the prophetic version of the story of Samuel and Saul and could nuance and supplement it where necessary with their own material. That Yahweh had rejected Saul and elected David they, too, could affirm. Yet in 1 Sam. 16:1–13 there is no mention made of a dynasty descending from David. The unit, in fact, recalls 1 Sam. 9:3—10:16 with its emphasis on the authoritative role of the prophet and Yahweh's spirit and is, as we have seen, a parallel piece to 10:17–27 as well. In this David seems to stand in the same position Saul first did when called by prophet and deity. Such emphases and nuances of the prophetic perspective would not be wholly acceptable as they stood and would have to be blunted by a royal perspective that centered on David as the elect of Yahweh and founder of a dynasty which stood under unqualified divine blessing. In short, 1 Sam. 16:1–13 would have to move onto 2 Samuel 7. The distance between them was mediated by Davidic material that was now integrated into the latter part of the older story of Saul. David, as Samuel did in his own way before him, would now come to over-shadow Saul. Saul would serve as a foil for the rising star of David, and at times David would so dominate the scene that Saul would slip wholly from view (21:2–16; 25:2–42; 27:1–12; 29—30). Elsewhere, Saul is on the sidelines, as in 1 Samuel 17, or only a threat to David (21:8; 23:7–13; 27:1), proving finally impotent. It must be noted that Samuel is also eased from the stage and with him the particular prophetic perspective he represents. After 1 Sam. 16:1–13, he appears only in 19:8–24 (where he saves David from Saul), 25:1 (an isolated notice of his death; cf. 28:3), and 28:13–19. All these are units from the older prophetic circle or the earlier tragedy. Each unit (save 25:1) serves to emphasize Saul's rejection in favor of David. The prophet has served his function and is allowed by the royalists to slip from view.

Throughout, David appears as Yahweh's elect, and because of this he is successful in whatever he does—even when driven by Saul from the royal court and family into the life of an outlaw, even when faced with grave dangers, even when in the apparent service of Israel's enemies, even when his own deeds are of questionable morality (21:2–10; 25:2–42). Material from the tragedy of King Saul dealing with David's entrance into Saul's entourage (17:12, 14, 17–23a, 24–25, 41, 48b, 50, 55–58; 18:2),[26] and his links with Jonathan (18:1, 3) and Michal (18:20, 22–24a, 26–27) could be taken up and in places (18:21a, 25b, 28–30)[27] made to underscore Saul's early responsibility for the break with David and the innocence of the latter. D. L. Jobling has demonstrated how the figure of Jonathan has served to effect the transition from Saul's rule to David's.[28] Already the rejection of Saul's dynasty in 1 Sam. 13:7b–15a calls special attention to Jonathan as the heir apparent in 1 Samuel 14. This is capitalized upon, we would suggest, by Judean royalists to legitimize the passage of kingship symbolically through the figure of Jonathan to David (18:4; 20:1—21:1; 23:15–18). Implicit in Jonathan's gift of robe, armor, and weapons (18:4), and finally explicit in solemn declaration (23:15–18), the emptying of Saul's son and heir into the figure of David is complete. Thus, in one version of the final meeting between Saul and David, the former even acknowledges the latter as his son, as innocent, and as the future king.

> "Is this your voice, my son David?" And Saul lifted up his voice and wept. He said to David, "You are more righteous than I; for you have repaid me good, whereas I have repaid you evil. And you have declared this day how you have dealt well with me, in that you did not kill me when Yahweh put me into your hands. For if a man finds his enemy, will he let him go away safe? So may Yahweh reward you with good for what you have done to me this day. And now, behold, I know that you shall surely be king, and that the kingdom of Israel shall be established in your hand." (1 Sam. 24:16–20).

The heirs and supporters of David could not ask for more from Israel's first king!

Two final encounters between the once and future kings now appear in 1 Samuel 24 and 26. The former, we suggest, reflects royalist tradition and was once part of a separate account of the rise of David. The latter is essentially from the ancient tragedy of King Saul but supplemented by royalist hands (26:9, 14b–16, 23–25a) to underscore aspects of a perspective already presented in chapter 24. Repetition reinforces the message. In these units, Yahweh's anointed is represented as sacred and thereby untouchable (26:9, 16; cf. 24:6, 10), a view to which the Davidic house could subscribe as once applied by David to Saul and now, by extention, to them.[29] David's innocence is stressed as well (26:23–24; cf. 24:11–15) in these two scenes.

Saul is now allowed to part from David for the last time as each man pursues the course clearly set for him. David moves unerringly onto the throne (1 Samuel 27; 29—30; 2 Sam. 1:1—5:10); Saul's path takes him to Endor and the heights of Mount Gilboa. While enveloping them in Davidic tradition, the royalists now allow units from the old tragedy of King Saul to speak for themselves (with the prophetic 1 Sam. 28:16–19a still in place). No doubt a certain stature could be allowed the fallen and rejected king in his death; for by the time of Hezekiah, when the material dealing with the rise of David was used to supplement and refocus the traditions received through northern prophetic hands, the house of Saul had long passed from the scene as a rival for kingship in Israel. Indeed, David's position as Saul's real successor had been now legitimized not only by prophetic designation but by the words and actions of Jonathan and even of Saul himself. As

David's lament in 2 Samuel 1 indicates, in royalist eyes there was a stature in the figure of Saul, visible clearly in his last days and in his death, that was not to be denied. Kings can recognize greatness in other kings, even those once their rivals. In this their perspective was not as harsh as that of the prophets.

In all this an ambiguity informs once more the depiction of Saul, for from a Davidic perspective he is finally less a villain than simply rejected, a foil for the man who stands under Yahweh's special blessing. With the exception of 1 Sam. 28:16–19a, Saul's crimes are less overtly against Yahweh than against David after 1 Samuel 15. But then the two, Yahweh and David, are linked by the closest of bonds in royalist eyes.[30] We might even suggest that in this perspective the door is reopened just a crack upon a dimension of the tragic vision. The fullest expression from royal Judean circles of the special relationship between the dynasty of David and Yahweh is found in 2 Sam. 7:8–16 (which seems to contain an ancient core supplemented by later hands; cf. 2 Sam. 23:1–7). This is a far cry from the perspective informing 1 Sam. 16:1–13. The deity's links with the Davidic house are now said to be everlasting (2 Sam. 7:13, 16), his *ḥesed* ("loyalty") unfailing (7:15, with an explicit contrast with his relationship with Saul), making room for chastisement (7:14) but never rejection (7:15). The only terminology adequate to express this is found in the relationship of a parent to a child (7:14a; father to son), and, however nuanced in terms of specific Israelite restrictions, these terms are used of no other mortal in the Hebraic tradition as they are with the Davidic line. Seeds are here sown that will grow slowly (see Hos. 11:1–4, 8–9; Isa. 55:3), and we cannot enter into the development of this potentially revolutionary complex of paternal symbols here. But we must note that at heart it fixes the fundamental relationship between deity and his elect on an unconditional basis, as one of life's givens, to be made of as the son will but a relationship never to be broken.

Saul was selected by Yahweh and then rejected. The royalists were willing to accept that and the reasons that northern prophetic traditions gave for it. But they did not dwell on them, and the disobedient Saul who withheld full and absolute loyalty from Yahweh is not explicitly found in 1 Samuel 16—31. We find, rather simply, the rejected king who falls into desperate madness and drives the innocent David from him into the arms of the enemy—but also drives him on a course that leads to the throne. The rejected Saul serves as a foil to the chosen David's rise. As rejected he cannot succeed, and his every deed becomes a mockery of his designs. In time he openly attempts to lay violent hands on David, only to fall into the relenting hands of the one he pursued. By contrast, the chosen David can only succeed, even against all designs set against him by Saul and circumstances.

Saul seems doomed again, and by a somewhat arbitrary force that can select one man as adopted son and in the process reject another. But this is muted by the prophetic perspective of the disobedient Saul and further by the fact that the royalist editor who combined the refocused tragedy of King Saul with his own traditions about the rise of David never lets us dwell long on the figure of Saul. His role is no longer played out on center stage as it was in the earlier strata. Saul is less tragic than pathetic in this new form.[31] Even in the death of Israel's first king the way is paved for the material preserved in 2 Samuel, and in this extended form the last word on Saul is uttered by David in his lament (2 Sam. 1:19–27).

It comes down to a matter of perspective, and in this the reader, in bringing a particular perspective to a text, must play a critical role. But it is a role shared with an author, or in this case with a series of creative figures who punctuate the developmental history of 1 Samuel. For each seeks to lend to the material received a distinct perspective by recasting what had been received and by adding distinct traditions. The tragic vision that informed the early stratum with its counterpart in the image of the savage god was transformed by prophetic hands and then further nuanced by Judean royalists. Through it all, however, the earliest tragic thrust was not wholly destroyed, and glimpses of it are still available to the sensitive reader. In 1 Samuel we have Israel's first sustained encounter with the tragic vision and evidence of attempts by circles within later Israel to absorb it through various transformations into the mainstream of Hebraic traditions. Visions of the just and/or loving god and his faithful spokesman or beloved royal son took pride of place over the savage god and the tragic hero.

NOTES

1. See J. L. Crenshaw, "*Wisdom in Israel* by Gerhard von Rad," *RSR* 2 (1976): 6–12. In his more recent work *Old Testament Wisdom: An Introduction* (Atlanta: John Knox Press, 1981), 42–65, Crenshaw extends his criticism to imply that evidence for the attribution of a wide range of wisdom materials to the period of Solomon is slight.

2. W. Lee Humphreys, "Rise and Fall of King Saul," 74–90.

3. Ibid.

4. Ibid.

5. W. Brueggemann, *In Man We Trust: The Neglected Side of Biblical Faith* (Richmond: John Knox Press, 1972).

6. See G. von Rad, "The Beginnings of Historical Writing in Ancient Israel," in *The Problem of the Hexateuch and Other Essays* (New York: McGraw-Hill, 1966; reprint, London: SCM Press, 1983), 166–204; R. N. Whybray, *The Succession Narrative*, SBT 2d ser., 9 (London: SCM Press, 1968); D. M. Gunn, *The Story of King David: Genre and Interpretation*, JSOTMS 6 (Sheffield: Univ. of Sheffield Press, 1978).

7. See von Rad, "The Joseph Narrative and Ancient Wisdom," in *The Problem of the Hexateuch and Other Essays*, 292–300; idem, *Genesis: A Commentary*, OTL (Philadelphia: Westminster Press, 1972); G. W. Coats, *From Canaan to Egypt: Structural and Theological Context for the Joseph Story*, CBQ Monograph Series 4 (Washington: Catholic Univ. of America Press, 1976); W. L. Humphreys, "The Joseph Story," *IDB Supplementary Volume* (Nashville: Abington Press, 1976), 491–93; H. C. Schmitt, *Die nichpriesterliche Josephgeschichte: Ein Beitrag zur neuesten Pentateuchkritik*, BZAW 154 (Berlin: Walter de Gruyter, 1980).

8. Von Rad, "The Joseph Narrative," 296–99.

9. Von Rad, "The Form-Critical Problem of the Hexateuch," in *The Problem of the Hexateuch and Other Essays*, 50–74; idem, *Genesis*, passim; W. Brueggemann, "David and His Theologian," *CBQ* 30 (1968): 156–81; H. W. Wolff, "The Kergyma of the Yahwist," *Int.* 20 (1966): 131–58; and the commentaries, especially those on Genesis, generally.

10. See below, 73–79.

11. Compare the events involving David, Bathsheba, and Uriah the Hittite. One needs little imagination to feel the impact of this story in the court of Solomon!

12. G. von Rad, *Wisdom in Israel* (Nashville: Abingdon Press, 1972); W. L. Humphreys, *Crisis and Story: Introduction to the Old Testament* (Palo Alto, Calif.: Mayfield, 1979) chap. 4; G. E. Bryce, *A Legacy of Wisdom: The Egyptian Contribution to the Wisdom of Israel* (Lewisburg, Pa.: Bucknell Univ. Press, 1979) especially chaps. 6 and 7.

13. As well as on the fate of the ark in disastrous encounters with the Philistines, which we do not consider here.

14. If, as some suggest, this story once told of Saul's birth, the irony of its appropriation into Samuel's story only underscores the radical recasting of the older material by later hands.

15. B. C. Birch, *The Rise of the Israelite Monarchy: The Growth and Development of 1 Samuel 7—15*, SBLDS 27 (Missoula, Mont.: Scholars Press, 1976), 11–21. See also Humphreys, "From Tragic Hero to Villain," 95–117, for the argument developed in this chapter.

16. See M. C. Lind, *Yahweh Is a Warrior* (Scottdale, Pa.: Herald Press, 1980) for the development of this theme in the Hebraic tradition.

17. Birch, *Rise of the Israelite Monarchy*, 21–29.

18. Ibid., 29–42.

19. Ibid., 42–54.

20. Gunn, *Fate of King Saul,* chap. 2.

21. Ibid., chap. 3.

22. S. De Vries, "David's Victory Over the Philistine as Saga and as Legend," *JBL* 92 (1973): 23–36.

23. Ibid.

24. Humphreys, "From Tragic Hero to Villain."

25. See J. Bright, *A History of Israel* (Philadelphia: Westminster Press, 1981), 278–88.

26. See the analysis of De Vries, "David's Victory."

27. Verse 21b is a redactional link with 18:17–19, an alternative to 18:20–27.

28. D. L. Jobling, "Saul's Fall and Jonathan's Rise: Tradition and Redaction in 1 Samuel," *JBL* 95 (1976): 367–76; idem, "Jonathan: A Structural Study in 1 Samuel," in *The Sense of Biblical Narrative,* JSOTMS 7 (Sheffield: JSOT Press, 1978), 6–8, 11.

29. By the time of Hezekiah, a genuine Saulidic threat to Davidic claims would not exist.

30. 1 Samuel comes to us now as part of the extended "Deuteronomistic history" (Joshua—2 Kings) which takes its overarching perspective from the Book of Deuteronomy. However, it is generally recognized that in the case of 1 and 2 Samuel evidence for the hand of these later historians is slight. Only in 1 Sam. 8:8–22) and 1 Samuel 12 (especially vv. 5–25) have sustained contributions been made by them. Elsewhere brief notes (7:3–4, 13–14; 13:1; 20:11–17, 23, 40–42; 25:28–31) serve to accent concerns shared by them and the material at hand. See Birch, *Rise of the Israelite Monarchy;* McCarter, *1 Samuel,* passim.

31. Robert Alter has called attention to the clarity of motive and purpose behind Saul's actions in the narrative. Motive is supplied him, either in a report of his thoughts or directly by the narrator. At points he is made to appear almost blundering in the obviousness of his intentions, especially as he seeks to destroy David by setting apparently impossible conditions on the latter's marriage to his daughters. David, of course, succeeds in every case. By contrast, throughout the material we learn much of David's words and deeds, but for him motive is not supplied, and a constant ambiguity surrounds his activities. See Robert Alter, *The Art of Biblical Narrative* (New York: Basic Books, 1981), 114–30.

CHAPTER 4

Flirtations with
the Tragic Vision

In the previous two chapters, we have considered in some detail an early encounter between the tragic vision and the Hebraic heritage. We have seen that the tragic vision with its implied or explicit theological dimensions stands ill at ease within the more characteristic range of ancient Israelite religious traditions. It stands in marked contrast to other products of the united monarchy and in even sharper contrast to the early prophetic vision of Yahweh's ways with humankind. As the savage god of the tragic vision was transformed, the tragic hero became, of necessity, a villain. It seems clear that, when standing within more normative traditions, the ancient Israelite could not unblinkingly look into the harsh light cast by the tragic vision. Nor could its particular glare shed light on Israel's religious landscape for very long or for many people.

Yet at least one expression of the tragic vision did emerge on Israelite soil, even if its author had cultural roots elsewhere. Could there have been others? It seems clear that if so they, too, did not remain unchanged. As the heritage has come down to us, it is in the figure of Saul that we have the closest depiction of a genuine tragic hero in the literary and religious traditions of ancient Israel. Here we will examine briefly a few other instances in which it could be suggested that tragic dimensions lie embedded in more normative Israelite perspective. We will be representative here rather than comprehensive, and we limit ourselves to material that is Israelite—that is, to material dated before the destruction of Jerusalem and the demise of the last traces of that ancient nation state in 587 B.C.E. We seek here not only to isolate possible glimpses of the tragic vision but also to note how they are comprehended and transformed by other hands and by the larger context in which they are now set. Broad patterns discerned in the previous two chapters shall serve as a guide.

SAMSON AND THE PHILISTINES

The stories about Samson are set only decades before the reign of Saul, and he also is caught up in a prolonged and destructive conflict with the Philistines. It is generally agreed that the material in Judges 13—16 reflects early encounters between Israel and its Philistine foes, who would continue to plague the young nation until David's successes some decades later. Composed of once individual narrative units, the Samson complex has recently received deserved appreciation for its literary quality and the artistry displayed in the interlocking of its composite parts.[1] One recent study[2] of this material devotes a chapter to the tragic dimensions of the material, although a large segment of that chapter[3] deals with the treatment of the figure of Samson at the hands of later tradition, from ben Sirah (who pointedly does not mention him) through Milton's portrayal of him in full tragic dress in his *Samson Agonistes*.

Actually, little ground for positive assessment of Samson as a tragic hero is provided by the biblical story itself, and I suggest that this is because the rollicking, impulsive, explosive biblical figure finally falls short of the tragic and becomes pathetic. (It is, referring to our earlier discussion, the necessary balance between fate and flaw that sustains the tragic vision.) To place undue weight on one or the other without holding a balance or tension between them is to capitulate to the pathetic on the one hand and the working out of justice on the other.[4]

In a generally sensitive treatment of the Samson material, J. L. Crenshaw seems hard pressed to fit it into a tragic mold that just will not contain it. He tends to understand the tragic as simply something terrible that happens to someone, not only Samson, but his Timnite bride, her unfortunate little sister, the men of Ashkelon, and even the youth who guided Samson to the pillars of Dagon's temple. All are brought under this definition of the tragic.[5] However, some of these figures are sketched with but the fewest strokes necessary to allow them to serve their brief function in the story and then vanish. They seem to be agents rather than full characters.[6] A definition of the tragic that takes in so many and varied figures in one brief narrative falls far short of its classical potential. This Crenshaw seems to recognize in his statement that "these figures approach a tragic dimension, if one understands the term broadly to refer to destiny over which one has no control."[7] We have seen in our introductory discussion that this is but one side of the tragic vision. These figures may indeed appear as driven, horribly unlucky, even doomed, but they hardly attain to the tragic. It is not clear, for example, in the case of the Timnite woman whether Crenshaw wishes to assert that she had a genuine choice when faced by the threats of Samson and the others at the marriage feast and that she made the wrong choice, or that the apparent choice was really no choice at all. If the "awful threat . . . really left her no option," could it be "plain that she made the wrong choice"?[8]

Samson, of course, does make choices, and his life's course is set by them. But these choices lack the elevated quality of those of the tragic hero. They rather too narrowly serve his self-interests (Judg. 14:1–3, 19; 15:1; 16:1) and almost always his strong appetite for women and violence. They spring from sexual passion or from a bravado that is at best narrowly concerned with securing his own honor (14:3, 8; 16:3, 23–28). His choices are those of the moment, at best akin to those facing Gilgamesh in the opening segments of the epic. Samson offers no sustained challenge to the limits that face human beings, nor is his life given over to a search for an unattainable boon that might enrich other men and women. Samson sees, desires, and takes, be it the woman from Timnah (14:1–3), an unnamed harlot at Gaza (16:1), or Delilah (16:4). In anger he strikes out, heedless of consequences (14:19; 15:8, 15). He serves no greater good, not even his fellow Israelites, in any sustained and conscious way—he is seen as a dangerous pest by the men of Judah (15:9–13). Saul fought Israel's wars, Oedipus sought to save his city stricken by plague, Gilgamesh decided to take his hard-won prize back to his fellow citizens of Uruk. By contrast, it is appropriate that a man whose life has been a series of blind lunges from lust to violence secures his greatest triumph only when finally actually blinded. Unlike Oedipus, however, his loss of sight seems not to bring deep insight in its train. His death is at his own hands, as is Saul's, but in Samson's case it seems only an unfortunate aspect of what is presented as his final and most successful attack on the Philistines and defense of his own honor: "So the dead whom he slew at his death were more than those whom he had slain during his life" (Judg. 16:30). His final prayer is to be avenged (16:28)!

It does seem possible to sustain the argument that Samson is fated, that he is set on a course that must bring him to blindness, chains, and even death in a pagan temple. As the text now stands in loose Deuteronomistic dress, it is the deity, whose overriding intent it is to find occasion for a quarrel with the Philistines, who sets this course

(14:4). Samson's life is devoted from conception to Yahweh and is under the guidance of his spirit, a spirit that seems to feed on this man's desire for women and combat (13:25—14:4; 14:6, 19; 15:14). He is indeed driven. Crenshaw comments on this depiction of the deity:

> Yahweh itches for a fight; he can hardly wait to provoke a skirmish with the Philistines. His spirit seizes Samson and wreaks havoc among the enemy. It matters little to him whether the Timnite, Ashkelonites or Gazites are innocent victims of Samson's fury. . . . This God delights in ritual purity. . . . [ethical] behavior is irrelevant to this God. . . . Samson can murder and fornicate, and God will continue to bless him. But let him cut off his hair, and God will depart from him forthwith.[9]

From the Philistine perspective, at least, this is the very image of an arbitrary and savage god—and from Samson's perspective as well, for a moment of vexed weakness (in the lap of a woman) leads to his rejection by his god. The will of hero and deity only come together in Samson's last prayer, as a hero's desire for revenge at last coincides as never before with the deity's desire to destroy masses of Philistines. The cost is the hero's life.

Seeds for the tragic vision may be here in this depiction of the deity, but they fail to take root and blossom when mixed with the figure of Samson. The balance of fate and flaw is not sustained, for Samson's failings are all too human and narrow. Moreover, they arise more from deep-seated passion than from conscious choice. Only at the very end does he appear in anything like the stature of the genuine tragic hero, as his deed becomes more deliberate (16:26—27), and a fuller recognition of his situation is manifest in both his prayer (16:28) and his last words: "Let me die with the Philistines" (16:30). Crenshaw rightly suggests that there is something comic in these words, a black and ironic note of humor.[10] Living with the Philistines, lusting after their women, in continued conflict with their men, he comes to an end that was all too predictable, and we, the audience, are in no significant way enlarged by it. We have been entertained and our tamer passions vicariously served by a well-told tale, but our vision of human potential and of limits placed on human being pressed to boundary situations has not been enlarged or clarified. Like his parents, we can only wish that he had stayed home and married a good Israelite girl (14:3). At best we can suggest that in the story of Samson Israelite tradition engaged in a flirtation with the tragic vision, but that, like Samson's own trysts, a deep romance or enlarged perspective failed to grow from it.

This failure was assured as the Samson story was taken up into the larger cycle of deliverer stories that comprise the heart of the Book of Judges and then into the pattern established by the Deuteronomistic historians. As the last of the saviors, Samson sits ill at ease with the likes of Ehud, Othniel, Deborah and Barak, Gideon, and even Jephthah. Samson's actions are presented as individual exploits; no Israelites accompany him. (In fact, in the one episode in which they appear, the men of Judah seem quite willing to be rid of him.) He acts simply for himself and not to deliver others. His successes are decidedly limited. As the last of the deliverers, he stands near the end of a depiction of the history of the federation that seems designed to chronicle its steady disintegration. Just before Samson appears Jephthah, the outlaw-made-savior, whose victory over the Ammonites is won with an ill-conceived oath (11:30–31) which costs his daughter her life (11:34–40) and later sparks a civil war (12:1–6). Then follows the material in chapters 17—21, appended to the Book of Judges, as well as 1 Samuel 1—6. In all this there is a steady increase in both internal disintegration and external menace facing the federation. Only Samuel, in time (1 Samuel 7), and then a fundamental change in the nation's structure will save Israel. Samson's story becomes an episode in a larger pattern of disintegration, part of a large typology ultimately designed to comprehend Israel's later fall into Babylonian hands.

As the Samson story is caught up in the continuing cycle of apostasy, punishment, and deliverance, whose classic statement seems found in Judg. 2:11–23 (see also 3:7–9, etc.), its image of the savage deity is blunted. His action through Samson against the Philistines is related to a broader course of action that is tied to covenant Israel's obedience (13:1) and the deity's willingness to deliver his people again and again (15:20; 16:31), even if the Samson material is rather roughly forced into this pattern. We are reminded of the treatment that the early tragedy of King Saul received from northern prophetic hands, whose secure place in the early lineage of Deuteronomistic circles is generally recognized. Once again we find ourselves viewing events from the perspective of a just and sovereign deity whose relationship with his people cannot accommodate a hero of tragic potential, whether that potential is realized or not.

As Crenshaw suggests,[11] it is in Milton's treatment of Samson that the seeds of tragic potential found in the biblical story reach full bloom. This is done through refocusing and a number of additions to the material. In Milton's work, which centers on Samson's last day, the hero becomes reflective as he reviews his life through a final encounter with Delilah (now made his wife) and a Philistine giant named Harapha. The basic questions of divine justice are made to emerge in dialogue between Samson's father, Manoah, and others. The biblical Samson who seems at points pathetically driven like an animal becomes in Milton's hands a finely cast psychological portrait of human suffering and responsibility, of a man caught up in the ambiguity of the quest for the good. By focusing solely on the one moment in Samson's life when in the biblical form of the material the potential for the tragic is greatest, and by designing the work around critical encounters not found in the Bible but providing a self-reflective dimension permitting the hero's pain to be transformed into deep human suffering and recognition of human limits, Milton cultivates the dim tragic potential found in his biblical source. But the route that must be followed in doing this sets a marked course away from the Hebraic traditions about Samson and the context in which they were preserved. The last words of Milton's Samson reveal this fundamental transformation of the biblical material:

> Brethren, farewell; your company along
> I will not wish, lest it perhaps offend them
> To see me girt with friends; and how the sight
> Of me as of a common enemy,
> So dreaded once, may now exasperate them,
> I know not. Lords are lordiest in their wine;
> And the well-feasted priest then soonest fired
> With zeal, if aught religion seem concerned;
> No less the people, on their holy-days,
> Impetuous, insolent, unquenchable.
> Happen what may, of me expect to hear
> Nothing dishonorable, impure, unworthy
> Our God, our Law, my nation, or myself;
> The last of me or no I cannot warrant.[12]

Milton's view is based on Samson's last words in Judges 16, words laced with ironic bemusement and some bitterness: "Let me die with the Philistines." Comparison with the tragedy of King Saul shows that the basic forms are there: death by his own hand in battle with the Philistines, fear of mockery at enemy hands, burial by those devoted to him. But the biblical Samson is not able to fill those forms, as was King Saul, with tragic stature. In a later age, at the hands of one who came himself to know blindness and prison, one who himself experienced unhappy relationships with women, and one deeply informed by his Hellenic as well as Hebraic heritage, the figure of Samson would attain that stature.

GENESIS 2—3

Milton drew inspiration not only from the story of Samson; in Genesis 2—3, he found a springboard for his greatest work, *Paradise Lost*. In these chapters of Genesis, an Israelite flirtation with the tragic is to be seen as well. Marked affinities between *The Gilgamesh Epic* and the story of the Garden and the so-called "Fall" should also alert us to this.[13]

Genesis 2—3 inaugurates an epic presentation of Israel's earliest history, set against a backdrop that depicts the human situation as perceived by the Yahwist, whom current scholarship generally sets in the period of Solomonic rule and in the context of the royal establishment. The Yahwist presents the human situation as characterized by harsh discord and destructive tension on all levels—humankind in disobedience and rebellion against the creator, at odds with and cut off from a natural world which no longer gives of its fruits unsparingly and can overwhelm at any moment, as well as human beings and whole communities in conflict with each other. This is all presented in a montage of scenes, many of which have striking affinities with material known to have been current elsewhere in the ancient Near East and especially the valley between the Tigris and Euphrates rivers. Genesis 2—3 sets the stage for this thematic prologue to Israel's history.

In brief we find there depicted a peaceable kingdom that was shattered because of human disobedience. Failure to observe a divine prohibition turned a cosmos whose essence was harmony between humanity, deity, and nature into a world torn by discord. Life-supporting patterns dissolve into virtual chaos. Blessing is transmuted into curse. The immediate cause is human refusal to acknowledge limits fixed by the deity.

The setting is a garden supplied by the creator with needed life-giving moisture and then an *'ādām* to till the ground. All that is needed to preserve and enrich life is found in this garden (Gen. 2:4b–9). Or so it appears! After a brief geographic notice about the central position of this life-giving garden in relation to the rest of the world, there appears a sudden notice of a limit placed on *'ādām*, on human being. In the garden *'ādām* may "freely eat of every tree of the garden." But this is immediately qualified—in fact, denied—in the next phrase: "But of the tree of the knowledge of good and evil you shall not eat, for in the day that you eat of it you shall die" (Gen. 2:17). Previously, in Gen. 2:9, two trees were given special notice—the tree of life and the tree of knowledge of good and evil—and now one is withheld from human beings. While not mentioned in vv. 16–17, the tree of life presumably remains available to 'ādām; only one tree is denied.[14] The narrative then moves on immediately to define the human situation in this garden: a superior relationship with the animal world is established (2:18–20), and 'ādām differentiated sexually as male (Adam from this point) and female.[15] "Naked and unashamed," they appear fully at home in this peaceable kingdom (2:23, 25).

All is in harmony at this point; there is no note of tension or discord.[16] Man and woman are childlike in their innocence. This dimension is stressed when Genesis 2—3 is read against the background of the opening Enkidu episodes in *The Gilgamesh Epic*. There we saw a childlike Enkidu at one with his natural surroundings and living in an eternal present. It was with the loss of sexual innocence that he matured and with this attained an almost godlike stature, as well as knowledge of human mortality. With full sexual development and awareness come physical and social maturity, a condition reflective of less developed social structures in which puberty, marking the onset of physical maturity for a girl or boy, brings marriage, procreation, and the assumption of adult roles, responsibilities, and privileges. After the encounter with the harlot, Enkidu leaves the creatures who were his companions and sets out on a path that will bring him to the city, to friendship with Gilgamesh, and in time to brooding over his imminent death as the ultimate limit placed by the gods on humankind. It should not surprise us that on one level of interpretation the "knowledge of good and evil" is linked with sexual awareness. Just before the scene in which the first human pair eat of this tree, we are told of their lack of shame at their nakedness (Gen. 2:25). Immediately upon their eating, we are told, "the eyes of both were opened, and they knew that they were naked" (3:7). Innocent nakedness becomes shame when faced with human nakedness. Sexual innocence becomes sexual awareness. Clearly, this is not the only level on which the "knowledge of good and evil" can be comprehended, for with sexual maturity comes a full range of human possibilities not available to the child, as well as the need to define new human limits.

Tension and a marked discord are soon found to be the further result of eating from this tree. Man blames woman when confronted by the deity; sexual difference becomes now a basis for exploitation and domination. The deity now curses the serpent, and through him the world of nature, because of human disobedience. Pain and toil will be the human fate, as well as submission on woman's part (an aspect of a cursed and not an ideal order) and enmity between humankind and the animal kingdom and even the earth itself. '*Ādām*, taken from the '*adāmāh* (ground), will now have to struggle with the ground for sustenance, struggle until it covers him and he merges with it again. Death is to be the humans' fate, and they are driven from the garden and from access to the tree of life (Gen. 3:22–24). The reason given is striking:

> Then the Lord God said, "Behold, the man has become like one of us, knowing good and evil; and now, lest he put forth his hand and take also of the tree of life, and eat, and live for ever." (Gen. 3:22)

Mortality alone seems to remain after this to distinguish human being from the gods, and the central theme of *The Gilgamesh Epic* appears once more.

Only at the end are we given the reason for the prohibition in Gen. 2:17. Or at least the deep reason is given, for the earliest statement that "on the day that you eat of it you shall die" proves to be true only because the deity drives them from the garden and the tree of life.[17] The proximate reason given in 2:17 gives way—indeed, they do not die "on that day"—to a deeper ultimate reason. Death is introduced to preserve a distinction between human and divine, and another way must be found to preserve humankind. There is irony in the fact that this mode of preservation is through the very power of human sexuality released through the violation of the divine prohibition. A life process is inaugurated that all audiences addressed by Genesis 2–3 must assume is natural: the child becomes adult and produces children in turn;[18] all of us must live, struggle, and procreate in a world too often alien—and then die. On the one hand this is the natural way, the way it is. But from another perspective it is flawed: it is not the way it once was and the way it might have been. A lost ideal, set at the beginning, essentially qualifies what now is. If we can relate Isa. 9:1–7 and 11:1–9 to the broad vision found here, this is an ideal to which humankind might return someday. It is striking that at the center of Isaiah's grand vision of the peaceable kingdom sits a little child (Isa. 9:5; 11:6, 8).

Yet one must wonder just how attractive this vision of lost and future innocence would really have been to the mature, cultured, and cosmopolitan epic historian or later prophet from the city of Jerusalem. Only the child seems at home in this ideal cosmos, it can be argued, and in that a note of ambiguity akin to that informing Enkidu's final review of his life informs the vision of the peaceable kingdom of Genesis 2 or Isaiah 9 and 11. Only as they can no longer live in Eden do human beings attain a status approaching the divine, and only then have they the full awareness of human mortality. In this respect we find ourselves caught up in what might be called a "paradox of the fortunate fall." Much was lost in the Fall but much gained as well, and the paradox centers on the inexorable link between the two. With wisdom and maturity comes death—awareness of it in *The Gilgamesh Epic,* actual loss of access to the tree of life in Genesis 3. A deep potential is there in 'ādām from the outset, just as an innocence is there. Its realization will come only at the terrible price of the loss of innocence and then of life itself. Yet for the reader of this story the situation into which man and woman move from the garden, however flawed and marred by death, has much to offer (as Enkidu must acknowledge). Growing up is good. We celebrate maturity and the wisdom that can grow in ourselves and others. New potential in life, friendships, enjoyment, and sensitivity are possible to the mature. But the first step down this path leads out of the garden, for it is the path of disobedience of god-given prohibitions, even if for mature humanity a necessary disobedience.

'Ādām—woman and then man—willfully chooses a course of action. It is a choice freely made, leading to what we celebrate as a potentially rich and rewarding course for human life, even if set within limits that are unacceptable. Speaking of the prohibition in Gen. 2:17, von Rad says:

> Even though God's prohibition was not at all oppressive, since all other trees were unreservedly declared free, it nevertheless placed before man decision and the serious question of obedience. To seek a purpose in the divine prohibitions, as exegetes have often done, is in our opinion not permissible; the question cannot be discussed. Nothing is said to indicate that God combined pedagogical intentions with this prohibition (in the sense of a "moral" development of man). On the contrary, one destroys the essential part of the story with such rationalistic explanations.[19]

Von Rad seems to want somehow to justify the divine prohibition—it was "not at all oppressive"—and also to say we cannot inquire about the basis for any justification. Yet we have seen that a purpose for the divine prohibition is indeed given after the fact in Gen. 3:22. And

Gen. 3:22 makes the situation here depicted much more paradoxical, ambiguous, and possibly tragic than the thrust of von Rad's remarks imply (and in this he represents the general tone of commentary on this material).[20] It becomes clear that the outcome of human disobedience was not simply destructive. A potential was released in *'ādām* that could only be blunted by denial of access to the tree of life.

Clear distinctions and separate levels are established within the cosmos in this account of the garden and "the Fall." First, the creation is distinct from the creator. Just as the animals are placed below *'ādām* (2:18–20), being named by *'ādām* (although like *'ādām* they are formed from the earth), *'ādām* is in turn distinct from Yahweh. Three tiers are established: deity, human being, nature. Yet, unlike the animals, *'ādām* can imagine a condition greater than its own and can aspire to it—and, when the way to it seems at hand, can grasp it. If this be hubris—and it has been so called[21]—it must be assessed in line with that of Gilgamesh in his quest for immortality, Oedipus in his quest for truth, or Saul in his desire to fill the role of ruler. Each instance of hubris involved a quest for what could not be had or, if had, only at a terrible price. The attributes found in the forbidden fruit by woman—"good for food . . . a delight to the eyes . . . desired to make one wise" (3:6)—are all attributes that human beings in every other circumstance would value. They are qualities of life's highest values and to be cherished as a source of joy. Thus, with deliberate consideration woman takes the fruit and eats and shares it with man (who shows less consideration and deliberation).

However, it cannot be said that *'ādām,* man or woman, attains a tragic stature in Genesis 2—3. The potential for tragedy is there, but that potential is blunted both by the humans' actions and attitudes following their disobedience and by the context in which the story is placed. When challenged by the deity, they seek to avoid responsibility for their deed: man places blame on woman and by clear implication on the deity; woman places blame on the serpent (3:12–13). And these are their last words (at least until the woman's in 4:1). From this point on they are passive receptors of whatever the deity dishes out. Having failed to dodge responsibility, they cease to act and become simply objects of action. Thus, by Gen. 4:1 they are once again in a partially restored harmony with the deity (however we are to understand the *'et-YHWH* of that verse). Oedipus submits to the will of the gods and to Creon in the end; Gilgamesh accepts in time the fate of all humankind; Saul faces knowingly his doom on Mount Gilboa, turning his own hand to the death foretold by Samuel. Yet in each case this comes only after prolonged struggle that wins each of them honor and a type of triumph even in necessary defeat. Oedipus does learn the dreaded truth; Gilgamesh has the plant of life for a time and demonstrates moral growth in having it; Saul leads his army into one more battle, as a king must against the enemy of his people. The cost in each case is terrible, but honor is due the tragic hero as well. 'Ādām makes no attempt to live to the fullest the potential discovered in the forbidden fruit. The humans make no move to "be as gods." Confronted by the deity they quickly capitulate, accepting the judgment the deity places on the situation. 'Ādām is not Prometheus. The divine assessment of the act as simply disobedience is accepted without question. The ultimate rightness of the prohibition in light of any belated justification is not questioned by them. Those who for an instant challenged the limitation placed on them by the deity quickly acknowledge their disobedience and become chastened creatures.

In standard interpretations, this element of simple disobedience is stressed by further justifying the divine prohibition as good for human being. Von Rad's attempt to do this—in the face of his own recognition that the basis for this is not given in the text—is an example. This is done in spite of the fact that, on the one hand, the limitation is finally justified by the deity primarily in terms of protection of the divine sphere from encroachment, and on the other, the apparent results of taking the fruit are values human beings affirm in the normal course of events. We are never told that the fruit is less than good for food or a delight to the eyes, and as the case of Enkidu makes clear, it brings a level of human maturity and wisdom that is in many ways to be valued. Yet this is played down not only by 'ādām's acceptance of the divine assessment of and judgment upon their deed but by the larger context in which the story is placed. Genesis 3 triggers for the Yahwist a series of destructive actions, as the remainder of the prehistory presents a typology of ever increasing disharmony, dissolution, and chaos within the created order: brother murders brother (Gen. 4:1–16), deities mate with mortals (Gen. 6:1–4), human violence sparks the unleashing of the flood (Genesis 6—9), a human attempt to gain fame and scale the heavens is thwarted and peoples set at odds (Gen. 11:1–11). Utilizing a range of motifs and stories from ancient Near Eastern lore, the Yahwist graphically depicts the human situation as he perceives it in which violence and chaos govern. The harmony of Genesis 2 has been shattered; curse has replaced blessing. In this the action of 'ādām in striving against limits placed on humankind becomes a first instance of disobedience, one in a long series of deeds that lead not only to chaos and death but also to further divine intervention and relenting. In this larger context the tragic vision cannot flourish. Divine justice, asserted if not demonstrated, justifies the actions of Yahweh, and a potential challenge to apparent arbitrary limits becomes a simple first case of disobedience that must be punished.

AN ARBITRARY GOD

We have seen that von Rad himself stresses that we must not seek to divine a purpose behind the prohibition in Genesis 2—3, even though he apparently goes on to do so. From the perspective of the deity, the considerations reflected in Gen. 3:22 seem clear enough and justified. But from the human perspective, as a limit on what humankind might be, the prohibition must appear arbitrary. The force of the prohibition is not to be doubted, but its justification is open to question. It is just this sort of questioning that the serpent sparks in the woman. This element of the arbitrary, of a fate or a limit fixed or imposed by the gods which demands of human beings acceptance of something less than full realization of their potential, is one way of considering one pole of the tragic vision. To stress arbitrariness in this depiction of the gods is not to deny their authority, their power to mold and order events and to shape the cosmos itself. It is, however, to challenge the principles by which they do this, to question the extent to which human being as it is and as it might be is taken into account. Even if most mortals appear willing and even eager to live within divinely prescribed limits, an occasional human figure will not. Then the potential for the tragic is present.

There are several points in the traditions of ancient Israel where extreme arbitrariness characterizes the actions of Yahweh. Three examples of this will engage our discussion of Israel's flirtations with the tragic vision.

Cain and Abel: Gen. 4:1–16

Several attempts are offered to provide reasons for and thereby justify Yahweh's acceptance of the offering of Abel but not that of Cain. All of them must falter before the striking silence of the story itself on just this critical matter. Generally, these attempts fall into two categories:[22] (1) the psychological, which places emphasis on the inner disposition of Cain as grudging in making his offering, thus rendering it unacceptable; (2) the external, in which Yahweh's supposed preference for blood offerings qualifies Abel's as superior. As an example of the former, N. Sarna says of the brothers:

> Abel demonstrated a quality of the heart and mind that Cain did not have. Abel's act of worship was an inward experience, an ungrudging, open-hearted concentrated devotion. Cain's noble purpose was sullied by the intrusion of the self, a defect that blocked the spiritual channels with God.[23]

From this Sarna is even able to draw out two basic concepts of Israelite religion.[24] E. A. Speiser seems to bring the two categories together as he states: "The manifest contrast is between the unstinted offering on the part of Abel and the minimal contribution of Cain."[25] Abel is unstinting, while Cain by implication is not so. And the quality of Abel's offering is superior, based on Speiser's translation of ûmēḥelbēhen as "finest" in Gen. 4:4.[26]

Von Rad is much more on the mark here when he observes that the narrative "refrains from making the decision for Abel and against Cain logically comprehensible."[27] He goes on to cite Exod. 33:19 as helpful in our understanding of this unit: "I will be gracious to whom I will be gracious, and will show mercy on whom I will show mercy." The lesson to be drawn from this story deals not with the external quality of one's sacrifice or one's inner disposition but with the freedom and authority of Yahweh over against all human standards or criteria. Human beings are to accept and recognize this; to do otherwise is to spark dissolution in the established order of things and to risk divine rebuke. But this seems just the point that many who treat Genesis 4 and similar material cannot accept. It is not the authority of the deity that they gainsay but the possibility that this authority might be exercised in disregard of human standards of the good and the right—indeed, in neglect of what might allow humans to realize fully their potential "to be." To fall short of full human potential through one's own failings is sad but just (one stews in one's own doings), but to be blocked by the deity for no apparent reason is to draw one toward the tragic vision.

It is, of course, impossible to suggest that Cain's response to the arbitrary divine rejection of his offering is in any way heroic, let alone tragic. Unlike Job, for example, he directs his rage not against the deity but against the innocent Abel. It is the situation that offers elements of tragic potential but potential that falls short of realization. The crassness of Cain's response denies in the end whatever tragic qualities the situation held, just as the stress on the destructive results of 'ādām's disobedience effectively thwarts the development of the tragic potential found in the situation shaped by the deity in Genesis 2—3. Once more, von Rad's brief insight is worth noting: "To keep the reader from horror, some resting point is granted him in the divine word of v. 6."[28] It is the reader who is to be shielded from "horror," a "horror" informing the situation itself, a "horror" provided by the potential in this vision of an arbitrary god. The reader is shielded by being quickly led away from the situation itself to the response of Cain and its destructive potential. Some responses will result in "acceptance" (so the RSV for s^e'ēt; others suggest "holding up the head"), but anger is not one of them. One must note that there is a terse ambiguity in the Hebrew of Gen. 4:7. It is not even clear on whose part the "acceptance" will take place. It could be that to be acceptable to the deity the human being must accept less than his or her full potential, and this may be the root of the anger that results. It is most revealing that interpretations of this story, as that of the disobedience of 'ādām, center on the destructive results of human actions, the lost peace and shattered cosmos, the fratricide and alienation. This is done to such an extent that qualities are found in the divine prohibition or in Cain's disposition for which the evidence in the material itself is decidedly minimal, if not wholly absent. The context into which this story is now set again reinforces this interpretative blunting of its tragic potential. Along with Genesis 2—3, it becomes one of a series of examples of human sin, illustrating the total breakdown of a once pristine cosmos. It is one more step on the road from shattered Eden to Abraham's call.

The Aqedah: *Gen. 22:1–19*

This striking episode in the cycle of traditions about Abraham has a complex prehistory of which only hints remain. The "testing" story *(Aqedah)* itself is often cited as a hallmark of Hebrew narrative style, with both a terseness that leaves much to the reader's imagination and the level of suspense built and held. As it stands, however, the suspense is vitiated to a degree by the opening statement that assures the reader that the spectacle about to unfold is only a test of Abraham by Yahweh. One is left to wonder, nonetheless, how far this test will be taken. The audience does have this information that is not shared by the actors in the story, however, and this attunes its perception of the events and modifies the potential horror implicit in the material itself.

A demand is imposed on Abraham by a deity who takes no apparent account of human parental feelings. The demand is un-

provoked and seems precisely designed to shatter in the most fundamental way this man's life. Abraham is told to offer as a sacrifice his
only son, and the context in which the story is now set only heightens
the terror by presenting the son as the offspring of his parents' old
age. He is the unexpected fulfillment of a promise long left in suspen-
sion, and there will be no more children. The blessings of greatness
and of many descendants that punctuate the story of Abraham (Gen.
12:1–3; 13:14–17; 15; etc.) depend on the now endangered life of this
son, this unique child ($y^e\hat{h}\hat{\imath}dk\bar{a}$), this one so loved by his father. To
Abraham no reason is given for this cruel demand; no larger purpose
seems served by this horrid request. Again the context reinforces the
horror by setting this at the end of a series of events involving
Abraham in which blessing and unqualified support is again and
again the keynote. Now against all expectations, against all past
patterns, comes this demand.

It is again to the credit of von Rad that he interprets this in the
context of divine freedom or arbitrariness, the freedom of the deity to
give and take, a freedom no mortal may challenge.[29] It must be noted
that other commentators seem more willing in this case to face the
arbitrary quality of this divine action. The reason may be in part the
sheer horror of the demand, but it may also lie in the manner in which
the story is formed limits the impact of this, both in the initial
observation that this is only a test and in the response of Abraham
(and his son) as well. After all, as physical and spiritual heirs of
Abraham through Isaac, we know that the sacrifice did not take place.

Once more, the potential for tragedy is quickly blunted; for again it
is the situation that contains the elements of tragedy, while the action
of the hero denies them realization. This time it is not, however, the
crassness of the hero's action as in the case of Cain; rather, it is his
total and unqualified obedience to the demand. The measured pace
of the narrative bespeaks itself of a determination to do all that is
asked. Abraham's commitment to this deity is absolute, his obedience unqualified. This hero demonstrates without a word of protest
that he is able to live within even these awful limits set by the deity.
No other course of action is considered, no countermeasures to save
his son, his line, and his identity itself. If necessary, Abraham wills
"not to be." And, of course, not only is the audience aware from the
outset that the demand is but a test, but in time they, with the hero
and the intended victim, all learn that it will not be carried to
completion. A substitute is provided for Isaac, and Abraham and his
god remain in full harmony as the latter blesses the old man with one

more renewal of the promise that has now begun to find fulfillment in the son whose life is spared. Calm obedience, like misdirected rage, can blunt the tragic vision.

David and Yahweh: 2 Samuel 24

"Again the anger of Yahweh was kindled against Israel, and he incited *(wayāset)* David against them, saying, 'Go, number Israel and Judah.'" So opens one of the units comprising an appendix to 2 Samuel. We are then told that David did as told, even over the objections of Joab. After David numbers his people, his conscience strikes him and he confesses that he has sinned. Three different forms of punishment are offered the king by his god, all of which would fall heavily upon the people. While the royal choice is never made fully clear, pestilence strikes Israel until Yahweh calls a halt to the devastation. The king then recognizes that his innocent people have borne the brunt of the punishment and asks that it fall upon him. This leads in turn to David's purchase of the threshing floor of Araunah, which could become the site of the temple in time.

From a number of aspects this brief unit remains less than clear, but it is not our intent to discuss its several problems in detail. Our attention centers first on the sentence, quoted above, with which it opens. It stands apart from a story that is clear without it, and it is not referred to again in the course of the narrative. Its function seems to be to place a once distinct story in a particular perspective, one that is in some ways close to that now governing the Samson stories. Yahweh bears ill will, this time against his own people, just as he did once against the Philistines. Acting on this, he incites people into action so that he may bring havoc upon them. He is successful in each case, even though it brings hardship on the ones incited and used by him. There are differences as well. In the case of the Samson story, the reason for Yahweh's anger against the Philistines is, at least as the material now stands, their afflicting Israel (Judg. 14:4). In 2 Sam. 24:1, no reason for Yahweh's anger is given, and it appears quite arbitrary. In fact, the narrative later implies through David's words that the people are suffering like innocent sheep (24:17). On the other hand, Samson suffers much more as the vehicle of Yahweh's vented anger than does David. When David calls for the hand of his god to be against him and his house and not against the people, he is told to buy a threshing floor and build there an altar to Yahweh. David incurs some expense but considerably less than that paid in the end by Samson.

It is the opening verse of 2 Samuel 24 that has attracted a great deal of attention (especially when compared with the version of this story in 1 Chronicles 21, which substitutes Satan for Yahweh), and this verse is clear: Yahweh is angry for reasons not specified, and he incites David to actions that must result in punishment on Israel. In isolation—and the sentence does stand in isolation—the action of the deity is again most arbitrary. Yahweh, it is implied, is presented driving David to a crime that will permit him to punish Israel, presumably as punishment of David.

It is once more the situation and the presentation of the deity that holds the potential for tragedy. Again, the quality of the action of the hero blunts this. David becomes the unwitting instrument of a Yahweh who seeks occasion against his people. Defiance of the norms of the community—and the numbering of the people is to be seen as just this—is not, in the context of 2 Sam. 24:1, a defiance of the deity who incites David to do this. In spite of this, David is willing to take upon himself the blame, and he quickly confesses his sin. Nowhere does he cry out as the one sinned against. All in all, 2 Sam. 24:1 interjects an awkward motif into a unit that at an earlier stage might well have dealt with the divine rebuke of an attempt by King David to exercise a royal right that flew in the face of such older federation traditions as are championed by Joab. In this case, David finds himself in the position of Saul, seeking to exercise the rights of kingship.

What then might be the function of 2 Sam. 24:1? Among other things, it functions to clear David of direct responsibility, if not punishment, for his census of Israel. While wrong, it was done at the behest of Yahweh for the deity's own reasons, which are not stated in the story. Drawing upon a vision of a deity who is at times arbitrary, a vision that informed a number of traditions current in the period of the united monarchy, this sentence serves with some clumsiness to exonerate David from primary responsibility for an act that violated older values, one that was linked with a pestilence that struck Israel early in David's reign. Once introduced in 24:1 to serve this role, the motif is quickly dropped before its full potential can be realized. Only the fine-tuned sensibilities of the chronicler would later find offense here.

JEREMIAH AS MAN IN MIDDLE

An apparently capricious or arbitrary quality in divine action or demands characterizes each of the units considered in this chapter.

We have treated them as instances of Israelite flirtation with the tragic vision. Actions are initiated and limits set by a deity showing little regard for human welfare, taking no central account of what is good or fulfilling for human beings, demonstrating no correlation with the moral quality of the lives or deeds of men and women. In these cases it is awkward to characterize this deity as just or loving, qualities that define the essence of Yahweh in more normative Israelite materials. The nature of the human response to this god and his demands varies, ranging from Cain's murder of his brother to Abraham's willingness to offer up his only and beloved son. In no case is the deity defied directly; no mortal stands up to the god on behalf of some violated human value. If a mortal strikes out at all it is against others, and submission comes too soon. Yet it is just this stance—of active challenge in the cause of some good that transcends the hero's own situation—that is at the heart of the tragic vision: Saul fights Israel's wars to the end; Oedipus strives to save his plagued Thebes; Gilgamesh seeks to gain immortality for himself and his fellows. The episodes considered in this chapter contain the seeds of tragedy, but in each case an essential human ingredient is lacking. Genuine hubris is absent. Not one mortal attains the stature of Saul.

This missing ingredient of bold human response is very nearly attained near the end of Israel's life as a nation in the life and ministry of Jeremiah. It is often noted that the paucity of information about those individuals who became prophets of Yahweh makes the reconstruction of their biographies impossible, and this prevents any full assessment of their distinct and human reactions to the message they had to deliver and its impact on those to whom they were sent. Evidence is slim for an assessment of how each one felt in the role of prophet. What evidence there is about the lives of the prophets is often oblique, in that it is preserved not to address our biographical concerns with the prophet as human being but, rather, to cast light on the word of Yahweh delivered through his prophet. Thus, for example, while the marriage of Hosea is presented from quite different perspectives in Hosea 1—3, questions still abound concerning the facts of the situation, leaving this as one of the cruxes of modern biblical scholarship. On the other hand, there is no essential uncertainty about the function of the symbol of a broken marriage in the depiction of the fractured relationship between deity and people in the oracles of Hosea. The biographical details are obscure, but the import of the broken marriage for the prophet's message is clear.

However, it is the case that with the later Israelite prophets, espe-

cially Jeremiah and Ezekiel, we do have at our disposal a far richer
and more varied body of apparent biographical and autobiographical
material than is the case with the earlier figures like Amos, Hosea,
Isaiah, and Micah. And even if the intent of this information is to cast
light on the word of Yahweh as delivered by the prophet—and this is
always why such notices are preseved in the tradition—it does indirectly cast some light on the situation of the man as well. Perhaps
most striking for our purposes is a series of challenges addressed by
Jeremiah to his god, often called his "laments."[30]

A. J. Heschel speaks of the prophet as "the man in the middle," the
man set between deity and people.[31] In the case of Israel's great
prophets, this generally means being caught in a position between
forces totally out of phase with each other. The people have rejected
their divine overlord, and the overlord is compelled to punish and
even destroy them. Somehow, however, the prophet must represent
each to the other. This especially means that the prophet is to be
identified not only with his god as speaker of the divine word, which
he must apply to the situation of his people, but he also must represent the people before their god (see, e.g., Jer. 21:2; 42:2–3). For in
important ways the prophet was with his people, as becomes clear
when we recognize that he exempts neither himself or others from the
disaster they recognize must come (see Jeremiah 45). Jeremiah rejects an offer from the Babylonian conqueror of Jerusalem that would
establish him in the victor's land. He elects rather to remain with his
shattered people (Jer. 40:1–6). More poignantly, following the capture of Jerusalem in 598, he utters a lament that betrays the full depth
of his attachment to his people:

> My grief is beyond healing,
>   my heart is sick within me.
> Hark, the cry of the daughter of my people
>   from the length and breadth of the land:
> "Is Yahweh not in Zion?
>   Is her King not in her?"
>
>   . . . .
>
> "The harvest is past, the summer is ended,
>   and we are not saved."
> For the wound of the daughter of my people is my heart wounded,
>   I mourn, and dismay has taken hold on me.
> Is there no balm in Gilead?
>   Is there no physician there?
> Why then has the health of the daughter of my people
>   not been restored?

O that my head were waters,
and my eyes a fountain of tears,
that I might weep day and night
for the slain of the daughter of my people!
(Jer. 8:18—9:1)

The year has gone round, but the mythic patterns of rebirth and renewal have not enveloped Jerusalem and its people, the city and folk whom Jeremiah had over and over to condemn in harshest terms.

This moving lament stands in striking contrast to his oracles, and in the gulf between them the terrible situation of the prophet as the man in the middle becomes apparent. Compelled by his god—seduced *(patah)* by him, as he will claim—to indict and pronounce sentence on his people, Jeremiah earns their scorn and bitter attack when it does not come to pass. Jeremiah feels betrayed by the god who called him to be his prophet and who overcame all hesitation on his part. As the object of both divine neglect and human attack, Jeremiah is utterly isolated, alone, disowned by his own kin, abandoned by all. He has been called by his god to a task that goes against his nature and will, and now from the abyss of loneliness and the rending of his psychic being he cries out in a set of unique prayers that come close to blasphemy (Jer. 11:18–23; 12:1–5; 15:10–11, 15–20; 17:14–18; 18:18–23; 20:7–11). In the course of his complaint, Yahweh is accused of supporting evil and failing to uphold the good. The deity seems in open attack against the just and those who live by his terms. In fact, the prime examples of this are found in the life of the prophet himself. It was to Yahweh that he devoted his life:

Thy words were found, and I ate them,
and thy words became to me a joy
and the delight of my heart;
for I am called by thy name,
Yahweh, God of hosts.
(Jer. 15:16)

His was a call to announce the destruction of his people. But over the years little happened. In the agony of betrayal he can only wish disaster for those over whom he had earlier wept, for those for whom he had not tears enough:

Therefore deliver up their children to famine;
give them over to the power of the sword,
let their wives become childless and widowed.
May their men meet death by pestilence,
their youths be slain by the sword in battle.

> May a cry be heard from their houses,
>   when thou bringest the marauder suddenly upon them!
> For they have dug a pit to take me,
>   and laid snares for my feet.
>
>   (Jer. 18:21–22)

His commitment to his role as prophet forbids any other attachments in life:

> I did not sit in the company of merrymakers,
>   nor did I rejoice;
> I sat alone, because thy hand was upon me,
>   for thou hadst filled me with indignation.
>
>   (Jer. 15:17)

It is a role he in no way sought; it was forced upon him in a contest in which he stood no chance.

> Yahweh, thou hast deceived me,
>   and I was deceived;
> thou are stronger than I,
>   and thou hast prevailed.
> I have become a laughingstock all the day;
>   everyone mocks me.
> For whenever I speak, I cry out,
>   I shout, "Violence and destruction!"
> For the word of Yahweh has become for me
>   a reproach and derision all day long.
>
>   (Jer. 20:7–8)

His days are filled with pain and mockery from which there is no escape:

> If I say, "I will not mention him,
>   or speak any more in his name,"
> there is in my heart as it were a burning fire
>   shut up in my bones,
> and I am weary with holding it in,
>   and I cannot.
>
>   (Jer. 20:9)

As a mere child he is selected by his god and placed in a position that could only destroy him. From Anathoth to Jerusalem, from village to city, temple, and palace, he is called to stand against kings and nations. He, like Saul, is compelled to stand between forces in deadly opposition to each other, attacked by one, abandoned by the other, left to be destroyed. He accepts the role of prophet and carries it out, all the while deeply grieved. His feelings are torn between sympathy for his people and anger at them, between shared grief with

his god for what he must do and betrayal as his words seem followed
by no action. He is ground up between god and people.

The result is the heart-rending cries from which we have cited. The
climax is reached in accusation against his god for the perversion of
justice, a challenge that is rarely found with such force in the Hebraic
tradition.

> Is evil a recompense for good?
>   Yet they have dug a pit for my life.
> Remember how I stood before thee
>   to speak good for them,
>   to turn away thy wrath from them.
>   (Jer. 18:20)

> Why is my pain unceasing,
>   my wound incurable,
>   refusing to be healed?
> Wilt thou be to me like a deceitful brook,
>   like waters that fail?
>   (Jer. 15:18)

> Why does the way of the wicked prosper?
>   Why do all who are treacherous thrive?
> Thou plantest them, and they take root;
>   they grow and bring forth fruit;
> thou art near in their mouth
>   and far from their heart.
>   (Jer. 12:1–2)

Pressed to the limits of human endurance and to the boundaries of
what it means to be a human being and a loyal Yahwist in the days just
prior to the death of his nation, the prophet lashes out in pain and
anger and deep-seated fear against an injustice that is never denied.

In time a response comes from the deity, but it is a strange reply.
On one level, it seems to sustain and renew the prophet's commitment to his task. On another, it seems no reply at all:

> "If you have raced with men on foot, and they have wearied you,
>   how will you compete with horses?
> And if in a safe land you fall down,
>   how will you do in the jungle of the Jordan?"
>   (Jer. 12:5)

> "If you return, I will restore you,
>   and you shall stand before me.
> If you utter what is precious, and not what is worthless,
>   you shall be as my mouth.

> They shall turn to you,
>   but you shall not turn to them.
> And I will make you to this people a fortified wall of bronze;
>   they will fight against you,
>   but they shall not prevail over you,
> for I am with you
>   to save you and deliver you."
>
> (Jer. 15:19–20)

"Get back," replies the deity, as his call is renewed, "get back to work."

Jeremiah does so. Like Elijah from Sinai, he sets his foot once more onto a path that will lead through many more years of suffering; a path that will take him through the terrible events of 587 B.C.E. and the turmoil of its aftermath; a path that will finally take him against his will down into Egypt with a people that seems determined consciously to reverse its sacred pilgrimage and story. His life will end pressed into unwilling service of survivors who seem intent on reversing their freedom march by going back into the land of Egypt (Jeremiah 44). For the remnant of his people, even the just god of the covenant is more than they can confront; how much more the savage god of the tragic vision?

Of the figures considered in this chapter, Jeremiah comes closest to the tragic, and perhaps more to the point, the tradition sustains him in this position as it did no other figure. His laments are preserved in all their force as attacks on a god who appears arbitrary and savage in his dealings with his servant, the prophet. Quite likely this is due to the fact that even here the interest of tradition is not on Jeremiah the man but on Jeremiah the vehicle for the word of Yahweh. It is increasingly recognized that in Jeremiah human prophet and divine word merge to such an extent that the fate of one is the fate of the other. The prophet becomes the word incarnate.[32] It is the word of Yahweh that forms the subject of the extended biographical and confessional material preserved in the Book of Jeremiah. It is the word of Yahweh that seizes and fills the prophet, that is isolated, terrified, that suffers and in the end is wholly rejected. The word of the deity is turned against itself, and the prophet's suffering is that of his god. As he is pressed to the boundary of meaningful existence, he mirrors his god's own dilemma, in which promise must become curse, and the sovereign Yahweh must turn on his own people, at last in total destruction. The life of the prophet is tragic as it is caught up in the life of this word. And it is so caught up in the most fundamental way:

Then Yahweh put forth his hand and touched my mouth;
and Yahweh said to me,
"Behold, I have put my words in your mouth.
See, I have set you this day over nations and over kingdoms,
to pluck up and to break down,
to destroy and to overthrow,
to build and to plant."

(Jer. 1:9–10)

He is unable to resist, however hard he tries. Nevertheless, he tries, as the outcries we have considered demonstrate. This sets him apart from others who, when pressed to the boundaries, draw back, or strike out obliquely in ways that are simply destructive, or accept their fate with a resignation that seems premature. We might wish that 'ādām had more to say about why they took the fruit, that Cain had demanded an explanation from the deity, that Abraham had resisted for at least a time for the sake of Isaac, that David had somewhat qualified his willingness to suffer for a crime he was incited to perform, that Samson had just once sat back and reflected on the forces that seemed to drive him throughout his life. In all these situations, we flirt with tragic potential, and in all we fall short. Jeremiah accepts in time his god-given task and does get back to work, but only after a challenge to his god that demonstrates the deep reflection and suffering of one pressed to human limits.

We might wish that the Yahwist had not been quite so precipitous in placing 'ādām and Cain in a context that spoke of human perversion of a once peaceful cosmos, a pattern of human-provoked curse that is modified only by divine relenting and blessing. We might also wish that Samson's story had not so readily been caught up into an account of the increasing disintegration of Israel. We would like more reflection on the first sentence in 2 Samuel 24. But in these cases the tradition seemed quite willing to blunt these flirtations with the tragic and to set them in the frame of reference controlled by a vision of a just and benevolent deity before whom human beings may stand as obedient or sinful, as justified and loved or indicted and sentenced, but not as tragic heroes. Only Jeremiah is allowed to approach tragedy.

In the aftermath of the death of the nation Israel in 587 B.C.E.—the crisis through which Jeremiah's long path was to take him—a new willingness to confront the tragic vision in its depth emerged within the Hebraic tradition. As the materials preserved in the Book of

Jeremiah already indicate, the time was right once again to be engaged by the tragic. In fact, the times demanded it!

NOTES

1. See J. L. Crenshaw, *Samson: A Secret Betrayed, a Vow Ignored* (Atlanta: John Knox Press, 1978); J. C. Exum, "Aspects of Symmetry and Balance in the Samson Saga," *JSOT* 19 (1981): 2–29.

2. Crenshaw, *Samson*, chap. 4. *- the tragic dimension*

3. Entitled "From Saint to Tragic Hero," 136–48.

4. We must be aware that we are dealing with degrees here and not wholly distinct categories—with a spectrum, with tragic in a middle range between the pathetic on one side and the just on the other. Thus, we might recognize a potential for the tragic in the figure of Samson that falls to the pathetic side of realization.

5. Crenshaw, *Samson*, 124–26.

6. See the definition of certain figures in a narrative as "agents" in A. Berlin, "Characterization in Biblical Narrative: David's Wives," *JSOT* 23 (1982): 69–85; idem, *Poetics and Interpretation of Biblical Narrative* (Sheffield: Almond Press, 1983), 23–42.

7. Crenshaw, *Samson*, 126.

8. Ibid., 124.

9. Ibid., 133.

10. Ibid., 129.

11. Ibid., 147–48.

12. *The Portable Milton*, ed. Douglas Bush (Baltimore: Penguin Books, 1976) 654–55.

13. I speak here of affinities to leave open the question of the dependence of the Genesis material on earlier Mesopotamian traditions and the nature of such dependence, should it exist. It is enough to note that both Genesis 2—3 and *The Gilgamesh Epic* deal with basic themes and that they fall within the same broad cultural sphere. In this regard, each sheds light upon the other.

14. See von Rad, *Genesis, ad loc.*, on the possible secondary inclusion of the tree of life, resulting in the difficult syntax of Gen. 2:9. The tree is not mentioned again until 3:22, 24. Yet it is there, critical to the resolution of the unit as it now stands: the life-sustaining garden is not so much destroyed by human action as human beings denied access to it. It remains as a lost ideal, someday to be attained again.

15. See P. Trible, *God and the Rhetoric of Sexuality*, OBT (Philadelphia: Fortress Press, 1978), chap. 3.

16. Unless this is found in the notice on marriage, which is quite possibly secondary. The child matures and takes a mate and new role, and as this happens the parents must redefine their role as well.

17. See also N. Frye, *The Great Code: The Bible and Literature* (New York: Harcourt Brace Jovanovich, 1982), 109: "The Genesis account permits itself a verse (3:22) in which God seems to be telling other gods that man is now 'one of us,' in a position to threaten their power unless they do some-

thing about it at once, with a break in the syntax that suggests genuine terror."

18. E. A. Speiser, *Genesis,* AB 1, 25, notes that in 3:9 Yahweh addressed Adam in the manner of a father to a child. But Adam is no longer a child!

19. Von Rad, *Genesis,* 78.

20. Cf. Westermann, *Genesis 1—11* (Minneapolis: Augsburg Publishing House, 1984), 304–5, who hints at tragic potential here.

21. Von Rad, *Genesis,* 88–90, speaks not only of hubris but of humankind setting its own standards, judging itself, and of "Titanism."

22. Ibid., 104.

23. N. M. Sarna, *Understanding Genesis* (New York: Schocken Books, 1970), 29.

24. Ibid., 29–30.

25. Speiser, *Genesis,* 30.

26. Ibid. This translation is assumed by Sarna as well, it appears, on 29.

27. Von Rad, *Genesis,* 104–5.

28. Ibid., 105.

29. Ibid., 244–45. See also the sensitive treatment of this unit by J. L. Crenshaw, *A Whirlpool of Torment: Israelite Traditions of God as an Oppressive Presence,* OBT (Philadelphia: Fortress Press, 1984), 9–30.

30. There is also a governing motif in the calls of several prophets (Isaiah 6; Jeremiah 1; Ezekiel 1—2; cf. Exodus 3) that points to a tragic potential in the situation faced by the one called. Each expresses a profound reluctance; he is not willing to take up the task, and excuses flow. Behind this is the realization that the prophet is to be caught up in a nexus of forces that are beyond human control or understanding. See also the case of Jonah. On Jeremiah's confessions, see Crenshaw, *Whirlpool,* 31–56.

31. A. J. Heschel, *The Prophets* (New York: Harper & Row, 1962).

32. See especially G. von Rad, *Old Testament Theology II* (New York: Harper & Row, 1965), 191–219.

CHAPTER 5

The Tragic Vision
and the Book of Job

THE MAN FROM UZ

The man from Uz was blameless. He was upright, a man of integrity, unrelenting in his devotion to his god. Job, the man to whom so much had been given, whose possessions could not be numbered, whose progeny were many, whose stature was unquestioned, who was esteemed by all—this man so blessed was blameless. It is important that we know this at the outset of his story and important that we know that we know it; for in time this will be called into question, will become the subject of extended and bitter debate. Job will be compelled to affirm this against all human opposition and then apparently have it challenged by the deity himself. Only then, perhaps, will it be affirmed. So, it is important that we know and remember and know that we know, that in the very first words of Job's story we have been told that Job is blameless, by an author who can report on the goings-on in heaven and whose words are affirmed by the deity (cf. Job 1:1; 8:2–3). Like the audience viewing an ancient Athenian tragedy, we read with knowledge that is either not shared by those players on stage or seriously called into question by them.

The Book of Job opens as a tight but artful narrative in objective and straightforward prose. Before we are plunged into the conflicting words and minds and perceptions of the characters of the drama, the author takes the position of a detached observer; as an omniscient narrator whose authority is unchallenged, he is even able to inform us of the debates and doings of the council of the deity itself. We begin with what is often called the "folk tale" of Job, presumably a well-known piece about the afflictions, suffering, and undiminished piety, the unquestioned devotion of the man from Uz.[1] In this way the stage is set for the drama that follows, and while much scholarly interest has centered on the possibility that the folk tale had a distinct origin and history apart from its present use, we must not overlook the critical role it plays as it opens our experience of the Book of Job. Even if not from the hand of the author of the poetic material that follows, it is assumed and expected that the reader will recall it as soon as the name Job appears. We must now attend to this tale that sets the stage for the drama of Job, for it is to this poetic masterwork, if anywhere, that literary critics who have sought the development of the tragic vision beyond and behind its Greek flowering have generally turned.[2]

The folk tale is articulated in a series of brief scenes that alternate between heaven and earth, between the establishment of Job and the council of Yahweh. We begin on earth and are introduced to Job, who, like Abraham, is rich in the livestock that defines a wealthy and respected semi-nomad. Unlike the first patriarch, Job is also blessed with sons, and he has three daughters as well (Job 1:1–3). He is the greatest of all the people of the east, and it is thereby implied that this is a tale not about a particular Israelite, and therefore couched in the specific terms of Hebraic religious traditions, but about any person anywhere. The work comes from the exile. The absence of anything specifically Hebraic—any mention of Yahweh's promise, the exodus, Sinai, law and covenant, of Zion and the temple and king, of promised land or exile, of all that filled the old songs and stories that could no longer, it appeared, be sung and told in exile (Psalm 137)—is striking in a piece whose themes are those of the Book of Job.

The conviviality of Job's children provides the occasion to underscore the hero's "piety."[3] After setting the stage on earth and establishing Job's piety and substance, the scene then moves to heaven and a gathering of Yahweh's assembly (called the "sons of God"), among whom is one who carries the title of "the Adversary" *(haśśāṭān)*. He provides a link between heaven and earth, for he has just come from moving about the latter. This provides an opening for the deity to boast of his servant Job, to assert that Job is all we have been told he is: blameless and pious. These facts are not challenged directly by the Adversary, but the basis for them is called into question: "'Does Job fear God for nought?'" (Job 1:9). Why shouldn't a man so blessed by the deity with all the good things of life demonstrate such piety? When the good have goods, it is easy for them to be good. Take everything from him, all that has blessed him and shaped his life, and even the pious man will curse his god.[4] Behind the Adversary's challenge lies a broader question: is piety possible? Is total and unqualified human allegiance to a deity possible, with no strings attached, no qualifiers, no conditions set or implied?

In brief, the answer of the folk tale is yes, as Job will demonstrate. As the scene moves back to earth, Job's situation has drastically changed. Job learns from a series of three messengers that all he possessed has been taken from him (1:13–19), and then from a fourth that his children are taken as well. Shattered by loss and grief, the pious Job nevertheless affirms his devotion to the deity, who, we have been clearly told, allowed the Adversary to do all this to his loyal servant (1:20–21). The first test set by the Adversary has been an unqualified success for the deity. This is brought home as the fourth scene opens like the second, in heaven and with the same give and take between deity and Adversary. Once more the challenge is offered, as if the wager were doubled. Touch his flesh,[5] dares the Adversary, and he will curse you. Once more the deity places Job in the power of his opponent; only his life is to be spared (for how can the dead show piety or the lack of it? How can they bless or curse the deity? How else could we know who won?). Job is suddenly and horribly afflicted. Even his wife urges him to curse his god and die, wondering at his firm insistence on his integrity (*tûmāh*, from the same root as *tām*, which is translated as "blameless" above). But she, not the deity, becomes the object of Job's rebuke: " 'Shall we receive good at the hand of God, and shall we not receive evil?' " It appears that the issue is resolved, for through "all this Job did not sin with his lips" (2:10).

Perhaps the issue at wager is resolved—Job's remains whole—but a host of other issues have crowded into the reader's mind. First, we must recognize that all that happens to Job in the folk tale happens at the initiative of the deity. The challenge of the Adversary provokes the deity, but Job's goods and children are taken and his body afflicted only as the deity allows this to happen. God afflicts the pious Job because the Adversary has called into question the basis for his piety. In the world of give and take between heavenly king and Adversary, Job's blamelessness makes him an apt target for attack. Only through his uprightness, integrity, and devotion to his god has he earned this attack—throughout, he is blameless. It is often said that the basic issue of the Book of Job is that of theodicy, the quality of divine rule of the cosmos. We must note that the issue of divine authority itself, or the fact of the deity's rule of the cosmos, is not in doubt. All that happens is from the hand of this god, and even the

Adversary's challenge can only lead to those specific actions which the deity permits. The assertion is made by Job himself: evil as well as good comes from the hand of this god. In his case unmerited, undeserved, and unjust evil falls upon a man who is, throughout, blameless.

Job is clearly caught up in a larger nexus of assertions and challenges, of claim and counterclaim, between deity and Adversary, that leads to his suffering and the loss of all that enriched his life and gave it meaning. Job is the victim of a wager fixed in heaven. By all that human beings must consider just and fair, by all we value as good and right, this is not just, this is not right. Is this, indeed, the way of the deity? Is this the nature of divine governance of the cosmos?[6] And what is the human being to do in this situation? Job's piety remains intact, but the cost is immense. Are there limits in the relationship between deity and human being? What does the fear of the god demand? Can (or should) a man or woman fear God for nought? All that gives texture and substance to his life—indeed, his very being—is taken from him. Job is pressed to the boundaries of human suffering in his attachment to this god who gives evil as well as good for reasons that have nothing to do with the quality of a human life or that are perversely related to it in an inverse (one might say demonic) way. The possibility of the savage vision of the god is laid bare in a way rarely encountered before in the Hebraic tradition and certainly not sustained since the work of the author of the tragedy of King Saul.

The stage is set for tragedy, but in the folk tale the tragic vision is not reached. The reason, as before in Israelite flirtations with the tragic, lies in the nature of the human response to this deity. Job seems under a dark fate and clearly at the mercy of forces beyond his comprehension or control. Yet Job remains passive throughout the story, accepting good and evil alike from the hand of a god to whom his devotion stands unblemished. He does not cry out, he does not even try to understand; he does not attempt to change the situation, to alter his fate. All that the deity allows the Adversary to dish out he takes without flinching. He can grieve (1:20), he can attend to his sores (2:8), but his only words in anger are directed toward his wife (2:10). He is angry because she suggests that he do something more, that there is more to being human than his passive acceptance and apparently mindless piety. The later Jewish tradition that links her with the Adversary as the final affliction set upon Job reveals indirectly deep insight in this respect. For behind the question of the Adversary—"Does Job fear God for nought?"—and behind his quips and challenges stands the broad issue of the nature of human being, of what it means to be human in this world created and sustained by this god. In Job's wife's assertion, the suggestion is made that there may be more to human being than passive acceptance of all the divine hand dishes out, even if being human means courting death in some situations, even if it means suicide. Is the Job of the folk tale to illustrate humanity at its best, or is there another model? How does one live with the savage god? This is precisely the range of questions raised by the tragic vision as it presses a heroic human being to the limits, to those boundary situations that define who and what we are, contexts in which for good or ill we find and enlarge ourselves. And while the blameless Job of the folk tale passively accepts the fate dealt him by the deity—as does Abraham, when faced with the terrible request that he offer his only and beloved son as a sacrifice—and falls short of the tragic vision, the Job of the poem that now follows will strike out both at three men who came to be with him in his suffering and at the god who caused it. He will strike back with words and with questions, some of the most dangerous in the Hebraic literary tradition.

JOB AND HIS FRIENDS

Poetic dialogues follow[7]—a harsh debate, the resolution of which the audience knows beforehand. Job is blameless: it has been driven home time and again in the scenes that set the stage for the poem of Job. In the ruin of the second test suggested and executed by the Adversary, Job is joined by three men identified as his friends: Eliphaz, Bildad, and Zophar. They are often called "comforters" by those who study the Book of Job, and the observation quickly follows that they proved false comforters and not friends at all. While not false, this is an observation too readily made. The three men care. They came to Job, and when they first saw him in his horrid condition, they "raised their voices and wept; and they rent their robes and sprinkled dust upon their heads toward heaven" (2:12). For seven days and nights, they sat grieving with Job in stunned silence. Thus, the author effects the transition from the old folk tale, which served to set his stage, to his poem, and in this he alerts us to the fact that the three are not to be lightly dismissed. In the cycle of dialogue that follows, he will give as much rhetorical effort to their words as those of Job, and the rhetorical resources of this poet are impressive. Their words would not be out of place in much of the Bible or Jewish or Christian piety.

The three have come to console and to comfort Job. The task that they have taken on is not an easy one. Recent studies have underscored for us the complexity of grief; it is marked by rough stages or layers ranging from rage through deep depression and, only in time, moving on to acceptance. Job is in the depths of grief, grief over the loss of his offspring and of a life that was full and rich, blessed and honored by all. The three respond first with silence, silence with their presence. They will be there with Job and not debase his suffering with easy answers or glib categories. In the silence of a human presence, they begin with sensitivity. Job first breaks the silence. The profundity of Job's grief first finds words in a lament which opens the poem. We are told that he "cursed the day of his birth" (3:1).

> "Let the day perish wherein I was born,
>   and the night which said,
>   'A man-child is conceived.'
> Let that day be darkness!
>   May God above not seek it,
>   nor light shine upon it."
>
> (Job 3:3–4)

He calls upon those whose words have power to raise up the very forces of chaos to curse that day:

> "Let those curse it who curse the day,
>   who are skilled to rouse up Leviathan.
> Let the stars of its dawn be dark;
>   let it hope for light, but have none,
>   nor see the eyelids of the morning;
> because it did not shut the doors of my mother's womb,
>   nor hide trouble from my eyes."
>
> (Job 3:8–10)

Death would be better than his present state:

> "Why is light given to him that is in misery,
>   and life to the bitter in soul,
> who long for death, but it comes not,
>   and dig for it more than for hid treasures;
> who rejoice exceedingly,
>   and are glad, when they find the grave?
> Why is light given to a man whose way is hid,
>   whom God has hedged in?
> For my sighing comes as my bread,
>   and my groanings are poured out like water.
> For the thing that I fear comes upon me,
>   and what I dread befalls me.

I am not at ease, nor am I quiet;
  I have no rest; but trouble comes."
                    (Job 3:20–26)

Job's grief is profound, and the task of his friends will not be an easy one. True comfort comes not through easy words and cheap sayings, let alone through a battery of pills or drugs or drinks that might still the disturbed and force decorum on those who might rightly want to rant and rave. True comfort demands empathy, a deep feeling for and with the bereaved, a recognition of and willingness to share the deep pain and horror called forth by a shattered life. It involves hard work: the work of slowly and painfully putting the pain and loss in some frame of reference that allows new life to grow where the old is lost, new meanings to replace shattered beliefs. A risk is involved in the work of the comforter, for empathy with another's pain and destroyed life can bring devastating suffering, and one may find treasured beliefs that have shaped and sustained life suddenly damaged beyond repair. It is this that Job's three friends risk, and the cost becomes clear as the debate turns into a debacle in its course of three cycles.

Job's lament is a beginning. The bereaved often first seem overcome by a pain and horror too deep and profound for words. But they struggle for words nevertheless, and the words can in time have an elegance and take on a demanding form (for example, see the Book of Lamentations). Job cries out with words powerful to stir up Leviathan, chaos itself; in time his own words will have the power to call from the deity a vision of Leviathan. Job's words allow Eliphaz to break silence as well, and his first words are both direct and sensitive:

"If one ventures a word with you,
  will you be offended?
Yet who can keep from speaking?
Behold, you have instructed many,
  and you have strengthened the weak hands.
Your words have upheld him who was stumbling,
  and you have made firm the feeble knees.
But now it has come to you, and you are impatient;
  it touches you, and you are dismayed.
Is not your fear of God your confidence,
  and the integrity of your ways your hope?"
                    (Job 4:2–6)

Yet his words sting Job. Both the depth of Job's pain and the difficulty of the task confronting his friends become apparent as, in even his first response to Eliphaz, Job turns on them in bitter attack. Those

who grieve are angry, and the anger is often directed toward the
nearest object at hand:

> "He who withholds kindness from a friend
>   forsakes the fear of the Almighty.
> My brethren are treacherous as a torrent-bed,   *W ADI S*
>   as freshets that pass away,
> which are dark with ice,
>   and where the snow hides itself.
> In time of heat they disappear;
>   when it is hot, they vanish from their place.
>
> . . . .
>
> They are disappointed because they were confident;
>   they come thither and are confounded.
> Such you have now become to me;
>   you see my calamity, and are afraid."
>
>   (Job 6:14–17, 20–21)

It is the apparent meaninglessness of what has befallen Job that
defines the challenge Job and his friends now face. Within what frame
of reference and belief, within what vision of human being and the
deity, can Job's shattered life find context and meaning? We must
remember that the folk tale has given us one: One possible conception of the deity that fits Job's situation is that of the savage god of the
tragic vision, of a deity who takes little account of the integrity of
individual lives or of the values and feelings of men or women, who
deals out weal and woe for reasons and in patterns that belie justice
or reason. To declare the deity unjust or unreasonable may simply be
to state that justice and reason—those grand visions of the human
imagination, those stirrings of the human heart—may have little to
do with the powers that shape and sustain the cosmos.

Whatever image of the god is set before us, there is the related
issue of how one is to respond to it. Again, the folk tale offers a
possibility in the pious and loyal Job, the servant who takes both good
and ill as they come without asking why or seeking larger meaning in
the context of the integrity or quality of his own life. Whether it is
blessing or curse that comes from the hand of the deity, the creature's
role in this perspective is to bless his or her god. The opening lament
of Job makes it immediately clear that this is not to be his response in
the poem. In his cursing the day of his birth and the night of his
conception, Job indirectly challenges the recognized source of all life.
By the end of the lament, it is clearly stated that it is his god who
hedges some human beings in, and the justice of this is called into

question. There is a rhythm in the lament that moves from a focus on Job's own situation and his wish for death to reflection on the nature of human life and the role of the deity in this, and then on to a closure of the one upon the other. Job 3:3–19 revolves around the rhetorical question, Why was I born, if to such a fate as this? Then in vv. 20–23 the focus changes, and a more objective tone is sounded in brief reflection on the disparity in the lives of some men (note the plural forms used), between the life they are forced to live and the death they seek, men whose lives have been hedged in by the deity. Then in vv. 24–26 the first person returns to close the circle, and it is made clear that Job views himself as one of those afflicted and hedged in and yet condemned to live. His own suffering stands behind the meditation of vv. 20–23. This movement from the personal to the contextual and then to the personal again holds Job in a tension that makes tragedy possible. He does not give into suicide lightly, however much he may wish for death. Nor does he simply stand back and intellectualize about the human situation. His despair is neither suicidal nor passive but "furious" and very much alive.

How are we to conceive of the deity? What are we to think of him? How are we to respond to his actions and shape a living space for ourselves in the cosmos he sustains? These questions inform the three cycles of debate. It is important that we note, through the invective that slices between the bereaved and his comforters, that they share some fundamental points of agreement. First, they agree that their god is or should be just. Somehow justice and the deity are to be linked in essential ways, and this must find reflection in the quality of life one is given by the deity. Only those whose lives fall short of the mark must suffer. Each individual life must reflect this pattern. The possibility of collective guilt and of punishment that can cut across the lives of the generations is but briefly entertained and dismissed by Job not to be raised again by the friends (8:1–7). Moreover, patterns of justice must be manifest in the life of the individual as that life is lived within the brackets provided by birth and death. No sudden transformations following death are to be allowed as explanations and alleviations for suffering experienced here and now. About all this there is little debate. The possibility of some sort of life following death is considered by Job in chapter 14 but quickly dismissed.[8] The suggestion that Job suffers because of the quality of the life of his children receives even less consideration.

Even though there is agreement that the deity is just and that this must find reflection in the rewards or punishments meted out to each life, the debate is bitter; for if the participants begin with a broad common ground of understanding, the perspective from which they view this ground is markedly different. Job observes it from the ash heap of his intense suffering. The friends must take it in from a perspective that seeks at once to encompass a strongly and generally held set of convictions about divine justice (8:3, 20–22; 4:7–11) and a friend who suffers deeply.

Struggle as the three may, no angle of vision is wide enough to take in both the just god and the suffering Job. And struggle as he will, Job cannot both entertain assertions of divine justice and maintain his integrity as at once suffering and blameless. To look upon the one is to turn one's back upon the other. Thus, as the invective and bitter tone of the debate intensifies, the friends turn their backs on Job as they defend their deeply held beliefs. Job for his part turns on them and then from them, as he cannot deny from his ash heap his integrity and suffering. They come in time to accuse Job of the most horrid of crimes as they defend their vision of their god. Job accuses them of an insensitivity that boggles the mind (12:2; 13:2–12; 16:2; 19:2–3) and lashes out at them, and then through and beyond them at the deity. By the end of the dialogue, the "'fear of God' " that Eliphaz at the outset suggested as the basis for Job's confidence (4:6) has turned to both terror and wrath, and the "'integrity of your [Job's] ways' " (4:6) has been denied over and over by all but Job and the still silent god. The gentle rebukes of Eliphaz have been replaced by the scorn and indictments of all three (5:1–16).

Still other points of agreement emerge, only to be viewed from perspectives so radically different that the discord is further aggravated. The fundamental distinction between the deity and mortal human beings is stressed:

"Can you find out the deep things of God?
Can you find out the limit of the Almighty?
It is higher than heaven—what can you do?
Deeper than Sheol—what can you know?
Its measure is longer than the earth,
and broader than the sea.
If he passes through, and imprisons,
and calls to judgment, who can hinder him?
For he knows worthless men;
when he sees iniquity, will he not consider it?
A stupid man will get understanding,
when a wild ass's colt is born a man."
(Job 11:7–12)

Job in his own way can reinforce the point made by Zophar: before this god, all men must appear of little worth:

"Truly I know that it is so:
    But how can a man be just before God?
If one wished to contend with him,
    one could not answer him once in a thousand times.
He is wise in heart, and mighty in strength
    —who has hardened himself against him, and succeeded?—
he who removes mountains, and they know it not,
    when he overturns them in his anger;
he who shakes the earth out of its place,
    and its pillars tremble;
who commands the sun, and it does not rise;
    who seals up the stars;
who alone stretched out the heavens,
    and trampled the waves of the sea;
who made the Bear and Orion,
    the Pleiades and the chambers of the south;
who does great things beyond understanding,
    and marvelous things without number.
Lo, he passes by me, and I see him not;
    he moves on, but I do not perceive him.
Behold, he snatches away; who can hinder him?
    Who will say to him, 'What doest thou'? "

                                            (Job 9:1–12)

From the viewpoint of the friends, this serves to undercut Job's claims of innocence: no man is innocent before this creator; in his pure light, all are sinners and of no account. Yes, agrees Job, the contest is clearly uneven, and the rules of the game—a game Job did not elect to play—are clearly designed by the deity to result in the utter defeat of all mortals. But that is in itself unfair, and it is perverse for a deity so powerful to take such an unhealthy interest and even delight in the affliction of one creature so small as Job. The gulf that separates divine and human is indeed so great that no mortal is able to cross it, and apparently the god is not willing to cross it. Job then pleads for some being who can come between the two of them, some arbitrator (*môkîaḥ*) who can bridge this gulf and bring them together. But there is none,[9] and Job is left with only his assertions of his integrity, ignored, it would appear, by the deity and scorned by his friends:

"My days are swifter than a runner;
    they flee away, they see no good.
They go by like skiffs of reed,
    like an eagle swooping on the prey.
If I say, 'I will forget my complaint,
    I will put off my sad countenance, and be of good cheer,'
I become afraid of all my suffering,
    for I know thou wilt not hold me innocent.

I shall be condemned;
   why then do I labor in vain?
If I wash myself with snow,
   and cleanse my hands with lye,
yet thou wilt plunge me into a pit,
   and my own clothes will abhor me.
For he is not a man, as I am, that I might answer him,
   that we should come to trial together.
There is no umpire between us,
   who might lay his hand upon us both.
Let him take his rod away from me,
   and let not dread of him terrify me.
Then I would speak without fear of him,
   for I am not so in myself."
(Job 9:25–35)

A movement has taken place as, in these words about and addressed to his god, Job begins to underscore the fact that the real struggle here is not between men but between one man and his god.

In terms of any cognitive gains, we end up just where we began the dialogue.[10] In terms of effect, however, there has been great movement. The friends have become hardened in their defense of their vision of their god and in their necessary denial of Job's integrity. Once more we must recognize that they are fighting for their religious lives: *their* "fear of God" and the "integrity of *their* ways" is at stake, and the very existence of the suffering Job has the radical potential to call all this into question. Their only defense is to deny their friend and turn from him, and if the denial of one human life is the price they must pay to preserve their theological structure, then so be it. Indeed, has not Job on his part bitterly turned on them:

"I have heard many such things;
   miserable comforters are you all.
Shall windy words have an end?
   Or what provokes you that you answer?"
(Job 16:2–3)

As he has from time to time throughout the dialogue, Job will soon turn from them one last time. From them he turns to the deity, and what was implied in the lament that broke his silence is openly voiced: Job knows the cause of his suffering. Job's god is accused by his "servant" of "a cosmic breach of faith."[11]

"Surely now God has worn me out;
   he has made desolate all my company.

. . . .

He has torn me in his wrath, and hated me;
   he has gnashed his teeth at me;
my adversary sharpens his eyes against me.

. . . .

God gives me up to the ungodly,
   and casts me into the hands of the wicked.
I was at ease, and he broke me asunder;
   he seized me by the neck and dashed me to pieces;
He set me up as his target,
   his archers surround me.

. . . .

He breaks me with breach upon breach;
   he runs upon me like a warrior.

. . . .

My face is red with weeping,
   and on my eyelids is deep darkness;
although there is no violence in my hands,
   and my prayer is pure."
                  (Job 16:7, 9, 11–14, 16–17)

What we the audience have known about him, Job continues to maintain as well: he is blameless.

THE COURT OF LAW AS A
CONTEXT FOR MEANING

Defense of the vision of a just god produced alienation between human beings. Suffering in the face of that vision resulted in terrible isolation and one man's lonely defense of his integrity against others who came to be wholly against him. As the human community in the persons of the three friends failed to console and comfort, Job in an act of extreme depression turned to the silent and distant source of all—his suffering and his only hope—to state once more his case. In Job 29–31 a grand oath of clearance is uttered by Job. First, he surveys his once blessed and happy state in which his integrity was respected by all. From this blessed man only blessing seemed to flow (chap. 29). Then the contrast with the present is depicted. Blessing has become curse, life is now a mockery of what he once was and death the only cure. Job is a pariah in the eyes of all (chap. 30). Then in chapter 31 he declares that he has done nothing to merit this and demands that his god come down and state his case against him. For what is he punished?

"Oh, that I had one to hear me!
    (Here is my signature! let the Almighty answer me!)
    Oh, that I had the indictment written by my adversary!
Surely I would carry it on my shoulder;
    I would bind it on me as a crown;
I would give him an account of all my steps;
    like a prince I would approach him.
If my land has cried out against me,
    and its furrows have wept together;
if I have eaten its yield without payment,
    and caused the death of its owners;
let thorns grow instead of wheat,
    and foul weeds instead of barley."

(Job 31:35–40)

Thus, the text tells us, the words of Job end.

At this moment, when Job turns for the last time from his failed comforters to address the deity directly, he shows himself ironically both at one with them in his basic presupposition about the nature of the deity and also at total odds with them. He will have no more words from them as he turns to address his god in a formal oath of clearance. Yet at the basis of this oath is a conviction that justice is the primary quality informing human relations with that god. He is suffering, of that there is no doubt. His god allows and even inflicts the pain. Suffering, especially in such extreme form, must be the result of human sin, it must correlate somehow with the quality of the life of the sufferer. Job, therefore, is being punished. Surely he has the right to know the crime he has committed to merit such punishment. Since it is the hand of the deity that punishes, it is now to the deity that he turns for notice of his crime. Sentence has come before indictment; Job now demands that he be indicted. Nothing less can be expected from a just god, and only to a just god can this grand appeal be made. In Job's eyes, his god is or should be just. In this Job and his rejected friends remain yet in agreement.

Nevertheless, he turns from them, for Job knows something more, something they have refused to recognize. From the roots of his own experience he knows that he merits no indictment that could justify a sentence as severe as that inflicted on him. He is blameless. We as audience knew this from the outset, and now Job himself asserts it with all the weight of a formal legal ceremony, for it is within the frame of reference of formal court proceedings that we must place Job's oath of clearance. Briefly, in such a context the accused is brought before representatives of the human community, typically the elders in the open space before the city gates, and charges are brought against the accused and examined. Evidence indicating the guilt or innocence of the accused is considered and, if possible, a verdict is rendered. Only then is sentence pronounced by the elders, who serve as judge and jury. The difficulty is that, in the case of Job, not only has sentence been executed without hearing or indictment by the divine judge, but when the life of the accused (accused by the very fact that he suffers, since only the guilty suffer at the hands of a just god) is examined by his friends, as elders representative of the human community, the results are inconclusive. In the eyes of his friends Job is guilty because he suffers, but of what he is guilty, they are unable to determine, even though they dredge a host of charges against him as their probe continues, and the debate becomes more and more bitter. This would happen from time to time in the court of law: inconclusive evidence would prevent the rendering of a verdict. In the ancient Near East, the trial was not, however, simply suspended but taken directly to the gods. Human inability to come to a decision resulted in the presenting of the case to the deity in the form of an oath sworn by the accused (and sometimes submission to an ordeal as well). The matter was then left with the deity to decide and to punish or not, as from the vantage point of the heavens guilt or innocence must be known. It was then out of the hands of the human community. Thus, Job's friends are not heard from again. Job has placed his case in the hands of the deity, and only the god can render a verdict.

Job has sworn in his tripartite oath that he is blameless, innocent. Ironically, in just this he becomes blameworthy from the perspective of the tragic vision. A hint of this is given in one of the few observations by the narrator, provided outside the prologue and epilogue. We are told in the transition into the words of one Elihu (Job 32:1–5) that Job was "righteous in his own eyes" (v. 1) and "made himself more righteous than god" (v. 2, au. trans.). These may be just the opinions of the three and of Elihu, but these notices may also reflect the first notice by the narrator that the evaluation given in Job 1:1 must be modified, especially as our angle of vision will soon change. Job is caught up in a nexus of inexplicable suffering that makes a mockery of his former life, and the human community in which for so long he was respected now forces him to lie in a bed he cannot and will not be made to fit. Pressed beyond the limits of meaningful human structuring of life, he strikes out for new meaning, new patterns by which to comprehend and find himself comprehended. He turns from his friends to his god and reaches out across the gulf that separates the divine from the human with his oath. He demands that the deity meet him, indict him—an indictment he would wear with honor—on Job's ground, on Job's side of the gulf, in the court of law. Job seeks to bring his god into a court of law and, on its terms, demands that the deity justify himself. "What have I done?" he cries. "Answer me!"

In this the blameless man becomes blameworthy, not in ordinary human terms but within the scope of hubris exemplified by the tragic hero. We have seen that this hubris is not linked to the small crimes of ordinary mortals but to Promethean attempts to be wholly self-defining and totally in control of one's life. Oedipus, for example, intended to rid his city of plague, and he claimed to know the course he must pursue, the way to pursue it, right from wrong, friend from foe. Saul knew what he must do to rule his nation and rid it of its enemies. Gilgamesh knew the facts of life and the way to immortality. They all knew but did not know. They knew and acted, but only in a constellation of forces and wills they but dimly perceived at first and came fully to perceive only in their fall. Thus, Job claims to know the ground on which he and his god can and must stand. He stakes out the turf on which the encounter between them must take place. He sets the questions to be answered, defines the terms in which the deity must justify himself. Then he demands that such a justification be given in the express terms he sets forth, on the very ground he defines.

Job poses his questions and in so doing defines the perspective from which the answer must come, for there is in the posing of questions this field-defining quality. Questions form their particular world of meaning; they stake out a frame of reference within which an answer must fit if it is to be an answer to the question. A response that fails to fit the frame of reference set by a question we call a non sequitur. A question which defines a field of meaning into which the one who must answer cannot fit we call loaded. Job earlier acknowledged the gulf between mortal and deity. Now he calls across that gulf and asks (demands!) that the god cross to him. In staking out the ground on which the god must stand to address him, he sets himself, if not equal to, then adequate to his god and equal to that task. He knows in what terms the god must answer; he will chart the course for the divine response. His frame of reference will be adequate, the stirrings of his heart will set the necessary ground. If not setting himself up as equal to his god, he claims to be at least equal to the task of defining the context into which his god must fit. In this lies the hubris of the tragic hero. Thus, the editorial clue to this in the opening of Job 32 which ends the human debate: "So these three men ceased to answer Job, *because he was righteous in his own eyes*" (32:1, italics added). This stands as an assessment of Job's oath and not simply a summary of the friend's assessment of him. Job's questions, contained in his oath of clearance, set as they are in the context of the court of law and informed by a vision of cosmic justice, will prove to be loaded when asked of the deity. For his god to be god, his answer to Job's questions must be a non sequitur.

Before we take up the deity's answer, however, we must pause, for a pause is demanded by the poem itself with the unexpected entrance of a man named Elihu. Within the legal frame of reference defined by Job's oath, human resources have been exhausted and the issue placed before the deity. Humans are to have no more to say about the matter, and the fact that one now does so should catch us up short, not, however, simply in quick pronouncement that the Elihu material (Job 32–37) is secondary, a wooden addition by the later hand of one who had some more to say. We should rather be caught up by Elihu's ill-timed entrance and jolted out of our perspective. Throughout the poem, we as audience have indeed been manipulated through a range of perspectives: from the alternation between heaven and earth in the folk tale, to the ash heap of Job's suffering and lament, and then to the bitter dialogue between Job and his comforters. We may not be sure from what perspective the issues are to be defined.[12] Then, in the oath of chapters 29—31, we are forcefully and fully drawn into Job's perspective as never before. His vision, presuppositions, and perspective come to govern us in his final rhetorical flourish in such a way that we may perceive the situation only with his eyes. The field of meaning defined by his questions and demand becomes our field, and it seems sufficient. Hubris can be seductive, and we as audience are drawn into the world defined by Job even as he seeks to draw his god into it as well.

In the young, bombastic, redundant, and sometimes insightful Elihu, we are jolted out of this perspective. Into a moment of solemn grandeur, in the face of a grand oath of innocence, onto the stage defined by Job, stumbles Elihu, angry at all concerned, saying he will be brief, saying it for line after line, deferring to his elders but allowing no one else a chance to speak, taking forever to get down to business. When he does, he seems simply to rehash in part what has already been said, with an added dash or two of his own insights. For our purposes now, interest lies not primarily in the substance of what he says but in what he does in saying it. We are jolted by Elihu out of

Job's world of meaning, and this is necessary. It is the essence of the tragic vision to press home to hero and audience that the cosmos the hero defines, large as it is, cannot be all-sufficient, that it is not large enough to take in heaven and earth. Job's frame of meaning cannot be all in all; Job must learn this, and so must we. Elihu's presence, ill-timed as his appearance is, prepares us for this lesson. As noted by those who attend carefully to what he says, Elihu both repeats some of what the friends and Job have said and anticipates dimensions of what the deity will say as well. Thus, we are quietly led to see that the truth can be multifaceted, found in varied constellations of questions, and viewed from diverse perspectives. With such insight the tragic vision can thrive. In the almost comic quality of Elihu, the stage is prepared for the deity to respond to Job and in this to affirm and then transcend the tragic vision.

THE TRAGIC VISION AFFIRMED

Out of the storm wind, the deity responds—so the narrator informs us. A barrage of questions follows, with the biting challenge to answer them:

> "Gird up your loins like a man,
>   I will question you, and you shall declare to me.
> Where were you when I laid the foundation of the earth?
>   Tell me, if you have understanding.
> Who determined its measurements—surely you know!
>   Or who stretched the line upon it?
> On what were its bases sunk,
>   or who laid its cornerstone,
> when the morning stars sang together,
>   and all the sons of God shouted for joy?
>
> . . . .
>
> Have you commanded the morning since your days began,
>   and caused the dawn to know its place . . . ?
>
> . . . .
>
> Have you entered into the springs of the sea,
>   or walked in the recesses of the deep?
> Have the gates of death been revealed to you,
>   or have you seen the gates of deep darkness?
>
> . . . .
>
> Where is the way to the dwelling of light,
>   and where is the place of darkness . . . ?
>
> . . . .

> Have you entered the storehouses of the snow,
> or have you seen the storehouses of the hail . . . ?
> (Job 38:3–7, 12, 16–17, 19, 22)

Blunt, ironic, impossible questions hurled at Job with the repeated challenge: "Declare, if you know all this" (38:18b). As has often been observed, the questions take no cognizance of Job's oath and demand, nor of the debate and the issues set out in it. Even the suffering of Job is ignored. It now becomes clearer that the whole book is built of questions, questions upon questions. Each set of questions undercuts the foundations for the earlier battery and presses us to new limits: from the Adversary's repartee—"Does Job fear God for nought?"—through Eliphaz's "Is not your fear of God your confidence?" and Job's "Why did I not die at birth? . . . Why is light given to him that is in misery?" to his implied "What have I done?" and now onto an endless series of brutal questions upon questions posed by the diety. New visions are now set before Job, and wide possibilities confront him that shatter the carefully defined ground of the law court that he established in his oath. ·

Assessments of the divine speeches are many,[13] but all must recognize that in some way or other that they are non sequiturs. They do not address the issues implied or set in what has come before, and especially in Job's oath of clearance. Even when Job seems to submit (40:3–5), the challenge continues, as the ground for the questions shifts from the created cosmos to the act of creation itself and the stilling of the monstrous forces of chaos whose image stands behind the creatures called Behemoth and Leviathan.[14] Powerful in their rhetoric, uncompromising as they never seem to end, the divine responses form a non sequitur. But this is not necessarily to pass a negative judgment upon them, for to loaded questions a non sequitur may be the only possible answer. As such, the questions posed by the deity become a judgment upon all questions earlier posed and upon the worlds of meaning they created.

First, the world of nature is hurled in Job's face: regular, perhaps, ordered but mysterious in its complexity, and beyond human comprehension and control. It is also a world in which the categories of the court of law, of justice and rights, simply do not apply. It is to the credit of M. Tsevat that this dimension of the divine speeches has been clearly underscored. The qualities of justice that inform the law court and define the dialogue between Job and his comforters, as well as his oath, are not applicable here. They do not apply to the natural world. Yet the deity is god of this realm as well; it is also a part of the created cosmos which he created and sustains. This, too, must enter into one's understanding of god. Then there is the very threat of chaos itself, with which the deity may play as with a pet on a string, a creature to be hunted for sport or its hide but before which human beings must stand impotent. This realm as well stands within the deity's sphere of control, and we must take account of that.

There are worlds beyond which the categories of justice and the right just do not apply, and over these the deity rules as well. From this new perspective, justice (being a construct of the human heart) must be recognized as sublime and profound only when kept in place—that is, when used as a construct for the assessment of human actions and the ordering of human communities. But justice, as Tsevat states, is too small a construct for the deity:

> Justice is not woven into the stuff of the universe nor is God occupied with its administration but it is an ideal to be realized by society and in it. As to God Himself, while the book does not say so explicitly, it does not exclude the possibility of God's obligating Himself to abide by human standards in regard to specific occasions and contexts. Thus God, while often the author of the standards of human conduct, is Himself bound by them only in exceptional cases.[15]

The universe and god assumed by Job and his friends in their dialogue and reaffirmed by Job in his oath of clearance is now shown to be too small. Job falls from the heights of bold and fearless self-affirmation of his rights hurled at the deity to repentance in dust and ashes (42:6). The traditions that were his heritage, his pride, and his boast, that grounded ultimate meaning, are shown to be too small. He can only now despise himself and say no more.

> "I know that thou canst do all things,
>   and that no purpose of thine can be thwarted.
> 'Who is this that hides counsel without knowledge?'
> Therefore I have uttered what I did not understand,
>   things too wonderful for me, which I did not know.
> 'Hear, and I will speak;
>   I will question you, and you declare to me.'
> I had heard of thee by the hearing of the ear,
>   but now my eye sees thee;
> therefore I despise myself,
>   and repent in dust and ashes."
>
> (Job 42:2–6)

Contrary to the notice at the end of his oath (31:40), Job's words have not ended. Yet they now seem the words of a new man. Where earlier he sought to define a world of meaning for his god to move into, now he responds to a world beyond all human patterns of meaning. It is the essence of the hubris of the tragic hero that it will take him beyond everyday worlds, within which most mortals fit with only occasional unease, to vistas that shatter those lesser worlds. Pride not only "goeth before the fall," it is necessary for the attainment of those heights that make the fall tragic.

Once more we must recognize that what Job seeks—affirmation of a cosmos with justice at its heart and the best of human imaginations standing at its center—is not lightly to be condemned. Job is blameless, and the justice he affirms ennobles most situations. The justice and right that Job strives to affirm represent human being at its best. The tragic hero is not a sinner within the narrow confines of that term, as it informs the diatribes of Job's friends. His quest is noble, but it cannot be all there is. When he makes it the basis for cosmic meaning—the frame into which all must fit, mortal and god alike— then hero and audience must experience its limitations and affirm that their lives are caught up in a larger nexus of forces that are finally beyond their comprehension and control and may not always ac- knowledge them and their values in any fundamental way. This is brought home with unique power in the endless questions that com- prise the divine speeches bringing the poem of Job to a close. Job represents the best in human being—a paradigm—as the folk tale, Eliphaz's opening words (4:3–4), and Job's own oath (chap. 29) make clear. But the paradigm he represents is finite. It cannot take in the cosmos and its creator. The creator cannot be measured by even the best of his creations, the finest of his servants. From the critical perspective formed by the divine speeches, even Job must stand not at the center but on the periphery of the cosmos; for this creator also takes note of and sustains mountain goats, hinds, wild asses, oxen, even ostriches, and the threat of chaos must always be held at bay.

The Yahweh speeches shift the ground or perspective in the poem of Job. Job, who called the deity to trial in the court of law, is in turn put on trial by the deity:

> "Gird up your loins like a man;
>   I will question you, and you declare to me.
> Will you even put me in the wrong?
>   Will you condemn me that you may be justified?
> Have you an arm like God,
>   and can you thunder with a voice like his?
>   (Job 40:7–9)

On this scale, the suffering of the blameless Job carries no ultimate significance and is ignored. This must be underscored against attempts by interpreters to read into the divine speeches hints of a providential divine order for ultimate good. In the cosmos affirmed by the creator in his response to Job, the good as perceived by human beings stands off-center and from profoundly significant points of view is now seen as tangential. Human frames of meaning are limited and at best partial, and interpreters of Job must face this as well. Tragedy is not for those who cannot accept unanswered and unanswerable questions, or answers that are questions. Nor is it for those who will not question. Easy answers deny Job the recognition and sympathy his suffering and integrity demand. The deity may perhaps ignore Job's agony; his fellow human beings cannot. It is precisely in this that his friends fail as comforters. We cannot be allowed to join them, for in Job's suffering we can all be enlarged—and the words of Sewall should be recalled: "The condition of suffering [is] the condition of pain and fear contemplated and spiritualized." We have allowed the hero his hubris; we have even been caught up in it. We must allow him his suffering and repentance as well. He began sitting "among the ashes"; at the end he repents "in dust and ashes." We must acknowledge the agony in each posture, even as we recognize the changes wrought. His suffering finally is bound to his attempt to move beyond the pain and fear expressed in his initial lament, to press to the boundaries of human existence, to extend those boundaries to take in the cosmos and its creator. In this he must fail and fall. But in this his and our world is enlarged even as we experience its limits.

THE TRAGIC VISION TRANSCENDED

Job thus rises above those who come to comfort him. The Book of Job ends not simply with the words of the hero in his final self-emptying. Two movements must be discussed.

The first takes place even in Job's last words, in a neglected but significant juxtaposition in what he states:

> "I had heard of thee by the hearing of the ear,
>   but now my eye sees thee;
> therefore I despise myself,
>   and repent in dust and ashes."
>
> (Job 42:5–6)

He "despises" himself—the rare Hebrew term seems possibly to denote a "melting into nothing." Yet the claim made in the words that immediately precede is not to be overlooked: "Now my eyes see thee [*rā'ātkā*]." The clear contrast is with former tradition, with what had been heard. Now Job can claim direct experience of the deity, if on the deity's own terms and in his way. But this is not all there is to this contrast. The movement is made from hearing (*šāmaʿ*) to seeing (*rā'āh*)—from, on the one hand, indirect to direct encounters with the deity. On the other hand, we move from a mode of expression with which the Hebraic tradition is comfortable when speaking of the deity to one with which it is decidedly uncomfortable and which it carefully protects against abuse. Throughout the Hebrew Bible, the deity is not only spoken of but the deity speaks and is heard and addressed in return; the tongue and ears form the medium of divine-human interaction. The eyes do not, not in the same way. The god may be said to see human beings, but precious few see the god. The few exceptions are carefully hedged about with qualifications. For example, it is the "glory" of Yahweh Moses asks to be shown in Exod. 33:18 and only his "back" which is seen by Moses (Exod. 33:23); twice (vv. 20 and 23) it is stressed that mortals cannot see Yahweh and live. Isaiah knows this well, as his reaction in his inaugural temple vision makes clear (Isa. 6:1–5), and it is possible he saw only the "skirt" (*šûl*) of his robe. Ezekiel sees what is carefully denoted as the "appearance" (*mareh*) of the "likeness" (*demût*) of the "glory of Yahweh" (see Ezek. 1:28b).

Job's assertion is in no way qualified: "Now my eye sees thee." Possibly he is unique; certainly he is placed in select company in this. Here the verb "to see" (*rā'āh*) is used without hedging or qualification regarding a mortal's experience of the deity. In Moses' "face to face" encounters with Yahweh, the verb is either "to speak" (*dibber*, Exod. 33:11) or "to know" (*yādaʿ*, Deut. 34:10), and Yahweh is the subject. Attempt as one might to tone down the force of this, the uniqueness of the claim made in Job's submission cannot be denied. Only here—in a work that too often, for all its recognized power, is consigned to the periphery of the Hebraic tradition—is the claim to see god simply made, without a qualifier. Only here, as the Hebraic tradition comes closest to a full confrontation with the vision of tragedy and the development of a tragic hero, does a man see god.

New experiences and boundaries now define Job's life with his god. He swings from seeing god to repentance in dust and ashes. No other figure lives within such a range, but then the tragic hero is like no other figure. Most men and women live in the middle ranges and safer registers; the tragic hero is here allowed heights not even his own hubris dared claim, heights attained even as he places himself once more in the ashes.

Just as the tragedies of classical Greece present the voice of the chorus as the last word, and just as Horatio or Octavius or Malcolm or Edgar delivers the last words in Shakespeare's tragedies, so in a prose transition back into the folk tale the last speech belongs not to the hero, but to the deity:

> After Yahweh had spoken these words to Job, Yahweh said to Eliphaz the Temanite: "My wrath is kindled against you and against your two friends; for you have not rightly spoken of me, as my servant Job has. Now therefore take seven bulls and seven rams, and go to my servant Job, and offer up for yourselves a burnt offering; and my servant Job shall pray for you, for I will accept his prayer not to deal with you according to your folly; for you have not rightly spoken to me, as my servant Job has." (Job 42:7–8, RSV revised)

From poetry back to prose, from drama composed of competing points of view expressed in direct speech (with minimal stage directions and editorial comment) to the omniscient narrator of the old folk tale: the words of Yahweh in 42:7–8 represent a transition that is often overlooked. As a type of anti-chorus, the friends of Job are summoned back on stage. But the relationships are now quite different. They were first introduced as "Job's three friends" (2:11), friends of the man whom his god had apparently forsaken. Now they are addressed as "you and . . . your two friends," and Job is once more designated by the deity as "my servant." At the outset they came to console and comfort him; now Job must pray for them, to deliver them from divine wrath. In this brief transition back to the folk tale, the tragedy of Job is transcended.

In the two best known cycles of Athenian tragedy, the Oresteian plays of Aeschylus and the Theban plays of Sophocles, a point is reached where the tragic vision is transcended by a vision that places human being—transformed and purged through suffering—at the center of the divine design for a moment. Thus, Athena of Athens brings resolution to the forces driving and hounding Orestes by reconciling the Furies and Apollo: the drive for vengeance and the horror of matricide. In the third play of the cycle, *The Eumenides*, justice, represented by Athens and Athena, reconciles the polar forces and releases the hero who was being torn between them. Sophocles's *Oedipus at Colonus,* a play that stands midway in the time frame of the cycle's story line but that came last in the course of Sophocles's life, allows Oedipus the god-given power to bless one human community in his selection of a place to die. The man so long under curse becomes a force for blessing in his mysterious death outside Athens. In like manner, the transition back to the folk tale of Job catches up the tragedy of the hero into a larger frame of reference.

The words of the deity in this transition are striking. Have not the three friends worn themselves out in the defense of their god against the outrages of this man Job? On what grounds are they now condemned?[17] I would suggest that the term *nᵉkônāh* carries much wider connotations than the usual translation of "what is right" when applied to the words of Job and the three. It is not simply the content of what they said—whether or not they have their facts right—that is connoted. It takes in the manner of their speaking as well, a connotation that I attempt to catch by translating the phrase as "you have not rightly spoken of me." What distinguishes the speeches of the three from those of Job is, first of all, a pattern of movement in Job's speech that is not present in the words of the friends. The three speak a great deal about their god; better, they speak about their understanding of their god. Job does this as well. But as he does so, a shift takes place, as he turns time and again from addressing his friends to addressing the deity.[18] In pain, in anger, in curse, in accusation, in despair, he turns time and again to the deity. He speaks not just about his god but to his god. Already, in his first response to Eliphaz, the transition from plural to singular, from friends to deity, is clear. Bitter invective cast at his friends—

> "Do you think that you can reprove words,
>   when the speech of a despairing man is wind?
> You would even cast lots over the fatherless,
>   and bargain over your friend.
> But now, be pleased to look at me;
>   for I will not lie to your face.
> Turn, I pray, let no wrong be done.
>   Turn now, my vindication is at stake."
>   (Job 6:26–29)

—becomes accusation of his god:

> "Remember that my life is a breath;
>   my eye will never again see good.
>
>   .   .   .   .
>
> Am I the sea, or a sea monster,
>   that thou settest a guard over me?

When I say, 'My bed will comfort me,
  my couch will ease my complaint,'
then thou dost scare me with dreams
  and terrify me with visions. . . .

. . . .

What is man, that thou dost make so much of him,
  and that thou dost set thy mind upon him,
dost visit him every morning,
  and test him every moment?
How long will thou not look away from me,
  nor let me alone till I swallow my spittle?"
               (Job 7:7, 12–14, 17–19)

Words about his god—

"For he is not a man, as I am, that I might answer him,
  that we should come to trial together.
There is no umpire between us,
  who might lay his hand upon us both.
Let him take his rod away from me,
  and let not dread of him terrify me.
Then I would speak without fear of him,
  for I am not so in myself."
               (Job 9:32–35)

—become words to his god:

"I will say to God, Do not condemn me;
  let me know why thou dost contend against me.
Does it seem good to thee to oppress,
  to despise the work of thy hands
  and favor the designs of the wicked?
Hast thou eyes of flesh?
  Dost thou see as man sees?"
               (Job 10:2–4)

This pattern reaches a crescendo, of course, as finally Job turns his back on his friends for the last time and lays his whole case before the deity in his final oath.

Thus, to Job comes the divine response and a vision claimed by no other. To the one who through his suffering rose above the time-tested and now worn dogmas of the friends, to the one who in so doing reached heights of hubris that must terrify all—to him alone the deity could speak. The full harshness of divine rebuke falls upon Job; his heroic hubris demands it. But in this he is also the only one in the drama to receive an answer from the deity. But then, he is the only one speaking to him. Once more the double edge of the tragic vision: as we have found, the hero is forced into a fall and yet is affirmed as heroic. Then, in the transition back to prose, the deity's words to the friends are few and permit no response on their part— they are not to speak to the god *of whom* but not *to whom* they spoke for so long. *Job* is now to pray for them! The object of their atten- tion—and in time, their scorn—is to be their savior.

Fallen and yet affirmed, rebuked and yet comprehended, heard and then seen as never before—the tragic vision is at once affirmed and transcended. S. L. Terrien has, in seminal studies on the Book of Job, placed the work in the context of the Babylonian exile, between the laments of Jeremiah and the visions expressed in the fourth servant song in the second Isaiah (Isa. 42:13—43:12).[19] The poem served, he suggests, as a paradrama, a substitute cult, for a people in exile, enacted especially at the time when recollection of the great festivals of the now dead nation would bring back with special poign- ancy the old songs that could no longer be sung (cf. Psalm 137) and the ancient stories that now only mocked. Here was a new drama that caught up their pain and fears and spiritualized them in deep suffer- ing. Their deep-seated questions, too terrible sometimes even to ask in isolation, found expression through this poem. The potential for tragedy inherent in their experience of the death of old Israel, the shattering of families, communities, and a nation, the identities torn apart, the apparent death of a religion—all are taken up in the figure of Job. They are taken up, affirmed, and then transcended. In the painful and angry struggle to ask questions that the mind has no frame of reference for asking—again, it is a book that builds ques- tions upon questions, new possibilities for a relationship with the deity are offered. It must be a relationship on the deity's terms, on his grounds, one in which all questions to and about the deity, his governance of the cosmos, and his ways with men and women, will be loaded questions. All human questions about and of the deity must be loaded.[20] But even in the non sequitur that becomes the only possible divine answer, there is an answer, one that is both a judgment under which all human beings and their questions must stand and a deepened contact with the one who answers. With new contact with the deity, new visions and the possibility of a future are offered. New webs of possible meaning, fleeting and mysterious and in no way denying the depths of suffering through which the human being may pass, are possible with a deity who in his own ways acknowledges the lives of heroes in exile, who sees and is seen. Those who suffer deeply can also save:

So Eliphaz the Temanite and Bildad the Shuhite and Zophar the
Naamathite went and did what Yahweh had told them; and Yahweh
accepted Job's prayer. (Job 42:9)

Taken only with chapters 1 and 2, Job 42:10–17 appear a simple
and even crass payoff by the deity who won his wager with the
Adversary. Restored goods and honor and servants and especially
children cannot make up for those lost, and new peace and blessing
cannot simply blot out long suffering and curse. In the face of what
the poem has allowed us to experience, this ending is unnecessary.
But in just this lies the value of this final notice. The restoration is
unnecessary; Job has already been at once crushed and affirmed by
the deity. Thus, this restoration is an act of grace, pure and simple.
The god who can in a moment afflict the blameless Job is also a god
who can restore those guilty of hubris. He can transform those who
stand against him into his own heroes. He makes tragic heroes his,
and they become those through whom reconciliation can be brought
to others. Even Job's new daughters—too often a burden on a family
in the economy of the ancient Near East—are here singled out as
special and as a source of blessing, whom their father blesses in turn
(42:13–15). Blessing as well as curse reside in the hands of this deity,
and his economy is not that of this world of men and women.

For the first time in the Hebraic tradition, we have tragedy confronted and transcended rather than blunted. In the case of the
tragedy of King Saul and in the other flirtations with the tragic we
have considered, the essential thrust of the material is blunted or
skewed by later reworking or location in a new context. In these cases
the ultimate force of the tragic vision is denied by a vision of a world
created and sustained by a just deity. In Job the tragic vision is
confronted. In a vision born of agony sparked by the death of a nation
and by exile, in the shattering of all regular aspects of life and the
apparent death of all symbols and structures, the author of Job
confronts the tragic vision in all its power and then asserts that
"tragedy is not enough." Tragedy is not denied: the tragic vision is
affirmed, even as it is transcended. A new sensibility emerges in the
Hebraic tradition that will have profound links with Western culture
and deep meaning for all heirs of old Israel. In the Book of Job we
have one of the most profound responses to the death of the nation
Israel, and beyond that to the human condition itself. If we set it at
the edge of our Hebraic heritage, we only impoverish what is ours to
cherish and pass on.

NOTES

1. The reference to Job along with Noah and Daniel in Ezek. 14:20 suggests that the story in some form such as this was well known. Simple mention of the name is enough to call up the necessary associations.

2. It should be noted that among those who work from within the perspective of the Hebraic traditions, theologians and biblical scholars generally, there is wide agreement that the high-water mark in the Hebrew Bible is in many ways the so-called "Second Isaiah" of Isaiah 40:55. Among those who stand within broader literary critical circles, the Book of Job is often highlighted. Both are products of the exile. Biblical critics and theologians are, of course, not insensitive to Job's merits, but the book is either described as sui generis or consigned to that stepchild of too much biblical study called "Wisdom," and thereby placed outside the mainstream of the Hebraic tradition.

3. I use this term, drawing upon the work of M. Tsevat, "The Meaning of the Book of Job," *HUCA* 37 (1966): 73–106; reprinted in J. L. Crenshaw, ed., *Studies in Ancient Israelite Wisdom* (New York: KTAV, 1976), 341–74, which I have found most informative, not to denote narrow attention to the details of worship or narrow religiosity but to a total pattern of character expressed by full allegiance to a deity, allegiance that will brook no rival. See also Crenshaw, *Whirlpool*, 57–75.

4. As a hint of the dangers that the soon-to-be-adopted posture of Job would come to have for later circles, the Hebrew text here (1:11; see also 2:5, 9) says not "curse" but "bless." Even the thought, the barest suggestion, that one might curse the deity was to be avoided. In such a context, the tragic vision would have great difficulty setting deep roots.

5. As in the first challenge, the Adversary uses what appear to be proverbial sayings in 1:9 and 2:4.

6. Job 1:1 introduces Job as a good and pious man, Job 1:2–3 as a man of substance. Any link between these facts—any causal connection between one's religious and ethical quality and the size of one's holdings—is at best left implicit by the narrator. While it is a link most in the Hebraic tradition might make, and most make today, we must note that it is the Adversary who first makes it explicit in vv. 9–10—this in a tale that clearly calls this connection into question.

7. See the commentaries generally for the arrangement of the three cycles and especially for suggestions on reconstruction of the disordered third cycle.

8. See Sewall, *Vision of Tragedy*, 67.

9. Job 19:25–27 is plagued with such textual problems that any certainty about its thrust is not possible.

10. The poem on the inaccessibility of wisdom found in Job 28 provides an apt comment on this state of affairs. If a secondary addition to the longer poem of Job, its placement is not arbitrary.

11. Sewall, *Vision of Tragedy*, 11.

12. Again, the poem in chapter 28 will only reinforce this with its notice on the limits of human wisdom.

13. See, e.g., S. L. Terrien, "The Book of Job: Introduction and Ex-

egesis," in *The Interpreter's Bible* (Nashville: Abingdon Press, 1954) *ad loc.* in vol. III; R. Gordis, *The Book of God and Man: A Study of Job* (Chicago: Univ. of Chicago Press, 1965) 117–32.

14. See Terrien, "Book of Job," 1186–90.

15. Tsevat, "Meaning," 104.

16. The term is reserved for very few in the Hebraic tradition: e.g., Moses (Josh. 1:1), Joshua (Josh. 24:29), David (2 Sam. 7:4).

17. J. Barr calls attention to the often overlooked verses that serve to take us back into the folk tale (cf. 2:11–13, that take us from folk tale to poem) in his essay "The Book of Job and Its Modern Interpreters," *BJRL* (1972): 28–46.

18. We must recognize that the comment of the deity in Job 42:7–8 takes in more than Job's last words of submission and self-emptying.

19. Terrien, "Book of Job," 877; idem, "Quelques remarques sur les affinités de Job avec le Deutéro-Esaie," *SVT* (1966): 295.

20. I am reminded of an episode from Elie Wiesel's *Night* on the power in questions. He speaks of his instruction at the hands of one called Moche the Beadle. Cf. my preface, xiii, and Elie Wiesel, *Night* (New York: Bantam Books, 1960), 2–3.

CHAPTER 6

Koheleth
and the Comic

For in much wisdom is much vexation.
and he who increases knowledge increases sorrow.

. . . .

Moreover I saw under the sun that in the place of justice,
even there was wickedness, and in the place of righteousness,
even there was wickedness. . . .
But he who is joined with all the living has hope, for a living
dog is better than a dead lion. For the living know that
they will die, but the dead know nothing . . .

(Eccles. 1:18; 3:16; 9:4–5)

TRAGEDY AND COMEDY

Tragedy and comedy form the twin masks of the Greek stage; the two seem at once joined and opposite.[1] Both are built upon a basic disjunction between some mortal's perception of the way things are or should be and the facts of the cosmos in which we live. We have seen that the essence of the hubris of the tragic hero is the imposition of his or her particular perspective on the cosmos and his or her initiating a course of action based on this, a perspective and pattern of action that the cosmos will not bear, that does not fit or contain it. The hero's point of view—often good and appropriate when in its place—is not all in all. Forces beyond the comprehension and control of men and women work hand in hand with a heroic willfulness to destroy precisely the one who takes life to its limits and confronts human boundary situations. As the Yahweh speeches make clear in Job, there are vast realms under the dominion of the deity in which human concerns and perspectives must remain peripheral. In tragedy, this fundamental disjunction between the human and the divine goes beyond the recognition of Joseph that the deity can, despite all

appearances to the contrary, bring ultimate good out of human de-
structiveness, and even beyond the deity's assertion in the Second
Isaiah that "as the heavens are higher than the earth, so are my ways
higher than your ways and my thoughts than your thoughts" (Isa.
55:9). For in the vision of the prophet of the exile, the ways and
thoughts of the deity are centered finally on human benefit: life and
peace and blessing will triumph in a world laced with human-initiated
death and curse and chaos.

Both the tragic and the comic build upon the gap between human
perceptions, values, knowledge, and control on the one hand, and the
nexus of forces that establish the ultimate context in which we live on
the other. The comic vision, however, allows human beings a place
nearer the center of that larger nexus that the tragic vision forbids.
Resolution comes in the case of each with the slow or sudden recognition of that larger nexus and of the limited nature of human awareness
up to that point. Resolution comes, in other words, when the characters in the drama come to share the knowledge that the audience has
possessed from the outset. The difference between the tragic and the
comic lies in the place accorded human beings. In the comic, the
resolution may come in spite of the intentions of the characters, but it
brings harmony, wholeness, peace, and life. Families are united, lines
of authority secured, kingdoms are at peace and rightfully ruled,
identities are clear, lovers are joined for life and misunderstandings
corrected. Second Isaiah, who probably lived through and was certainly sensitive to so much pain, was nevertheless speaking out of a
perspective that was, in the elevated sense, comic. The Hebraic
tradition, in fact, stands in this perspective, which is what makes this
prophet of the exile so grand a representative of it. In this perspective
it can even be asserted that the ending of the Book of Job transforms
that story into a comedy. This would carry greater conviction were it
not for the intensity and force of the poetry that comes between
prologue and epilogue. Indeed, it is in the deity's recognition of Job
as having "rightly spoken" that we first transcend the tragic vision,
and this renders the restoration that follows unlooked for and even
unnecessary (just the qualities that make it an act of grace!). For a
moment, a human being stands at the center of the divine desire for
restoration of relationship. Job's prayers and sacrifices will satisfy
those whose concern for divine justice requires some payment for
abuse committed, and the opportunity for this is provided as a loving
act of a relenting deity. In the comic vision the deity turns out to be

just and/or loving after all. In the Book of Job the comic transcends, but does not deny, the tragic.

Beyond this restoration of harmony, the comic also offers no hero upon which a drama can center and to whom the audience is drawn in awe and terror, for the tragic hero is indeed godlike in his or her hubris. At least heroes are godlike for a time, and it is as they come to discover that they are not gods that we move or are moved back from them, through the intrusion of an Elihu and other perspectives, through the words of the deity, through the final words of the chorus, or even through the terse and clipped pace of the narrative as at the end of the tragedy of King Saul or *The Gilgamesh Epic*. In comedy we are neither so intently drawn to the central figures nor must we regain our distance from them as the danger in their posture becomes clear. Few human heroes emerge fully formed from the Hebraic tradition. Only the tragic perspective permits the deepest engagement with a hero.

KOHELETH AND JOB

It is in this regard that it seems appropriate to devote some attention to the writings of one called "Koheleth" (the Hebrew title of Ecclesiastes, traditionally understood as "Teacher"). In the schema scholars design to organize the rich collection called the Bible, the Book of Koheleth (= Ecclesiastes) is often linked with the Book of Job: genus, wisdom; species, pessimistic or philosophic. Both books reflect a pattern found throughout the ancient world that seems to have grown out of and in reaction to the bold and positive affirmations that underlie the material found in much of the Book of Proverbs.[2] Job and Koheleth are thus linked, and yet they are so different. Job feels, and his book is laced with rage, terror, insistence, vehement affirmation, and denial. Passion is hardly evident in the words of Koheleth; he has burnt himself out, if passion once did infuse his earlier years (3:16; 11:9; 12:1–7 may be partial exceptions to this, in which rank injustice can still stir some depth of feeling).[3]

Koheleth in no way strikes out against the deity or the limits placed on human being. He maneuvers with what resources he has to find and accept what living room there is within those limits. He does not grow in the course of his writings, and he does not fall. His words, like his cosmos, go round and round in a circle, and we end as we began: "Vanity of vanities! All is vanity" (Eccles. 1:2; 12:8). This phrase and others of like tone[4] interlace the fine tapestry of his words as binding threads. Just as his opening hymn sings in steady measure of the endless circularity of the cosmos and of all in it (chap. 1), so the book moves round on itself with the steady pace of a procession toward the grave: "And the dust returns to the earth as it was, and the spirit returns to God who gave it. Vanity of vanities, says the Preacher; all is vanity" (Eccles. 12:7–8). From the opening statement that "there is nothing new under the sun"—a statement that tears the heart from more normative Hebraic traditions—to the closing allegory on the disintegration of human life in death, we are allowed to contemplate but not to feel; we observe with Koheleth, we chuckle at points[5] and shake our heads in dismay at others. But to care deeply and to show it, and then to struggle for something better, is not allowed. That, too, would be vanity.

KOHELETH'S COSMOS

The cosmos for Koheleth is the handiwork of a creator, and as such it is informed by patterns that are betrayed in the regularity of nature (1:3–7). There is time and season meet for all human activity (3:1–9). Cosmos, not chaos, is the context in which we live our lives. The bitterness comes from the fact that we must do this even in the face of a fundamental disjunction between the cosmos in its ordered essence and our often skewed perception of it. There may be "a time to be born and a time to die; a time to plant, and a time to pluck up what is planted; . . . a time to love, and a time to hate, a time for war, and a time for peace" (3:2, 8) but into the vital center of human being, the deity has placed something so that he cannot "find out what God has done from the beginning to the end: (3:11). Just what this is—be it intimations of "eternity," as the present MT pointing of the root ^cLM (^côlām) suggests, or a fatal finitude, as others would suggest on the basis of another form of $^cLM^6$—is not clear, but the result is plain enough. All may have beauty in its time, but the essential quality of a particular time or season is too often hidden from mortal sight and insight. The fundamental orders and patterns that inform our cosmos are just not available to human understanding, let alone control. On this level, the human creature is fatally flawed by the creator. From the human perspective too much happens by chance:

> For man does not know his time. Like fish which are taken in an evil net, and like birds which are caught in a snare, so the sons of men are snared at an evil time, when it suddenly falls upon them. (Eccles. 9:12)

Or else things occur in ways that do not correspond to the human perception of how they should be:

> Again I saw that under the sun the race is not to the swift, nor the battle
> to the strong, nor bread to the wise, nor riches to the intelligent, nor
> favor to the men of skill; but time and chance happen to them all.
> (Eccles. 9:11)

This verse epitomizes the one moment that is recognized as ap-
pointed for all, rich and poor, wise and foolish, all alike—death.
There is a perversely driven logic that can lead Koheleth from observations on the failure of justice in the world of men and women (3:16)
to the fact that all "go to one place; all are from the dust, and all turn
to dust again" (3:20). Not only can no person claim that death
distinguishes between human beings and beasts (3:19, 21), let alone
between human lives of distinct quality (9:2–3), but death robs life of
all genuine and lasting meaning and purpose. The only advantage the
living have over the dead is that the living know they will die and the
dead know not even that (9:4–5). Some advantage![7] Therefore, the
house of mourning, the lament, the sorrow, and the thoughts fixed on
the day of death more profitably exercise the imagination of the wise
than laughter, feasting, or the house of mirth (7:1–6). There is humor
in the way in which Koheleth can turn an old proverb about a live
dog's advantage over a dead lion into a parody on its intent, just as
there is in the gloomy adages he coins elsewhere. But this is a black
humor. Doctor Johnson once observed that "the prospect of death
wonderfully concentrates the mind."[8] It becomes an obsession for
Koheleth and the focus for a point of view that robs life of all ultimate
meaning. Even the good that he knows is there in life, and which
must be enjoyed by the wise man while he may, is no longer available
in any significant measure to the man now in the grip of old age and
with failing faculties (12:1–7; 11:6–10). His journey down life's path
has put more distance behind him than still lies before, and the
destination is too clearly in view.

Wisdom in Koheleth

Two thrusts in the sayings of Koheleth do modulate, if not finally
modify, this perspective. First, the wise teacher does not find himself
suddenly stripped of everything, shattered and seated on an ash heap
in pain and grief. He is a teacher with something to teach, and the
words of the epilogue, with their mild warning and bland assertions
(12:12–14), also state that he was skilled in the composition of wise
sayings that were found compelling by his students (12:9–11). We
have some examples of them in his own words (10:1—11:14).
We have to deal with two levels of wisdom in Koheleth. The first

level, which we might call the "medial" level, gives sound and hard-hitting advice, akin to that found in segments of Proverbs. Rules of thumb are available to the discerning, and they should be weighed and followed, not in a slavish manner, or as if they were words from heaven, but as rules of thumb behind which stand enough insight and experience to help one down the path through life. On this level, the wise have an advantage over the fool (2:13–14a; 7:19). But it is itself folly to believe that these rules of thumb carry any ultimate or lasting value. The wise may avoid a few pitfalls, but the path such wisdom eases is still the road to death that all must follow (2:14b–16). In death lies the annihilation of all that is of value and enriching in life:

> The dead know nothing, and they have no more reward; but the memory of them is lost. Their love and their hate and their envy have already perished, and they have no more for ever any share in all that is done under the sun. . . . for there is no work or thought or knowledge or wisdom in Sheol, to which you are going. (Eccles. 9:5–6, 10)

Again, it is death that is the cancer. Death prevents those hints of an order from leading to trust in the benevolence of the creator in the face of a mystery that overcomes all wisdom (cf. Prov. 16:1–4; 21:30–31). Death, in Koheleth's eyes, allows no final "God meant it for good."

At the second level, for those who recognize the rules of thumb and take them for what they are and no more, there is genuine pleasure to be had in this life. This, too, is built into the structure of the cosmos:

> There is nothing better for a man than that he should eat and drink, and find enjoyment in his toil. This also, I saw, is from the hand of God; for apart from him who can eat or who can have enjoyment? For to the man who pleases him God gives wisdom and knowledge and joy; but to the sinner he gives the work of gathering and heaping, only to give to one who pleases God. (Eccles. 2:24–26)

This, too, is from the hand of the god; but this, too, is also "vanity and feeding on the wind." The wise is the one who recognizes that there is pleasure to be had in life for a time and who therefore seeks it. The fool is the one who works and never asks, "For what am I working?" He amasses and never thinks about what the mass will be worth to him and to those who come after him. But the wise, the one who pleases the deity, also knows that pleasure is passing and not the basis for ultimate meaning in life. Pleasure gardens are not built for eternity. The strongest statement of this comes in a climactic passage in Eccles. 9:7–10:

Go, eat your bread with enjoyment, and drink your wine with a merry heart; for God has already approved what you do. Let your garments be always white; let not oil be lacking on your head. Enjoy life with the wife whom you love, all the days of your vain life which he has given you under the sun, because that is your portion in life and in your toil at which you toil under the sun. Whatever your hand finds to do, do it with your might; for there is no work or thought or knowledge or wisdom in Sheol, to which you are going.

The words recall those offered Gilgamesh by the deity Shamash and then by the ale-wife Siduri:

"Thou, Gilgamesh, let full be thy belly,
Make thou merry by day and by night.
Of each day make thou a feast of rejoicing,
Day and night dance thou and play!
Let thy garments be sparkling fresh,
Thy head be washed; bathe thou in water.
Pay heed to the little one that holds on to thy hand,
Let thy spouse delight in thy bosom!
For this is the task of mankind."

Gilgamesh was also on a journey, following a path that he hoped would lead to immortality. For him the stop at the tavern of Siduri was but a pause at a way station, for he would not allow her words to cut short his quest. Koheleth comes only to this saying through his assessment of the empty life which the deity has given mortals under the sun. He does not move beyond it; Gilgamesh's pause becomes his climax. In just this *The Gilgamesh Epic* approaches the tragic vision, while the Book of Koheleth falls clearly short. Intimations of immortality clearly define the quest of Gilgamesh, just as assertions of a fundamental justice in the cosmos do for Job. Justice is from the outset an illusion in the eyes of Koheleth (4:1; 7:15), and any intimations of immortality become for him simply certification of the fact of death (3:21).

At best, the rules of thumb and moments of pleasure to be found by the wise in a life of moderation (7:15–18) allow one to immerse oneself in the busy work that "God has given to the sons of men to be busy with" (3:10). Days may be filled with busy work, most of which is "drudgery" (*camal*) but interlaced with flashes of anesthetizing pleasure and finally the oblivion of death. Human life is played out on the edge of a cosmos more fully defined by observation of the larger world of nature, with its endless cycles in which no meaning or justice or final good is to be found for humankind (1:3–11). Koheleth begins his words with a meditation on these cycles of nature: sun, wind, seas, and generation replacing generation. Beyond this he comes into no contact with the deity; thus, "all things are full of weariness; a man cannot utter it" (1:8). Koheleth will go on uttering it for the bulk of his work, but that is all he will do. The Book of Job ends with a divinely sent vision of a world of nature that places his human and heroic point of view in a new perspective. Beyond and through this experience, the hero discovers new contact with the deity. If Koheleth is not wholly tranquilized by the everyday and the trivial, he is at least bemused to the point of resignation. He will seek nothing more, for he knows there is nothing more.

KOHELETH AND THE DEITY—SILENCE

Therefore, a silence pervades the Book of Koheleth. A great deal is said in the book about the deity, who is often referred to as "the god" *(hā'elōhîm)*. While this phrase is used elsewhere in Hebraic material to denote the deity and is not always used by Koheleth (cf. the use of the article in 3:10, 11), it seems that in the work of Koheleth it clearly serves to objectify the deity, to underscore his transcendence and the impossibility of all human contact with the divine. This is truly a *deus absconditus,* a "hidden or obscure deity." To *hā'elōhîm* of Koheleth, one does not sing or cry out in any way. Prayer or praise or lament or even anger is not directed to him (perhaps "it" is better)—thus, the divine silence that pervades the book. About the deity Koheleth speaks, but *to* him, never. This creator who set this cosmos in motion with all its complex and ultimately unknowable cycles within cycles and constellations of orders beyond comprehension, this deity is now masked by this creation. *Hā'elōhîm* is beyond this creation, while men and women are so very much caught up in it and in the wearisome cycles that lead from birth to death. One cannot address the other, for deity and humankind are in wholly distinct realms of being. Human beings are at the periphery of this cosmos; the values that inform human life are not finally in tune with cosmic rhythms— rhythms that move from life to death and catch us up as simply dust and the *rûaḥ* ("breath," "wind," "spirit") that enlivens it for a time (12:7). The essential structure of the cosmos is in dysfunction with the desires and values and dreams of the individual human being, and there is no deity to whom one can address words of hurt, anger, curse, or lament. Job turns from his friends to his god, time and again, and finally sets his whole case before the deity in direct and bold challenge. He looks to his god as the only possible mediator between him and his god. In this, relationship is reestablished between deity and humankind, and Job's last words are of petition for his friends. Koheleth's sayings are largely in the form of a daybook or journal, loosely organized at best, and thus seem addressed first of all to himself and only then to the larger but limited audience of his students, who must be warned to take them in the "proper" perspective (12:12).

The most striking silence in the Book of Koheleth, is not, however, the absence of human words addressed to the deity but of divine words addressed to human beings. Here, above all, the work stands apart from the Book of Job. There is no voice here from the storm, not even a still, small voice. The book ends as it began, with Koheleth's observation about the vanity of all. Hā'elōhîm, to whom Koheleth cannot speak, does not respond in any way. The stance of Koheleth permits no rebuke; there is no tragic fall, no thundering defeat, no destruction of a tragic hero. Only a profound silence will confront the one who knows that the imaginations of the human heart are not at the center of the cosmos and that it is vain to seek to make them so. We said that Job was Everyman, but this is only correct from one perspective. The Book of Job is not indeed about an Israelite or a Jew but about a human being before the deity. But Job rises above the stature of just any man; he is heroic. He rises above the position of his friends to new levels that at once terrify as they enlarge our vision of human potential, as well as of necessary limits. Koheleth does not enlarge our vision, even if he does bring the human situation into sharp focus. The limits are sharply etched in his words, but the overriding tone is of grim resignation, and this sets a frame of reference in which the tragic vision cannot flourish.

If the book falls short of the tragic, it falls short of the comic as well. Granted, we never feel for and with Koheleth as we do for and with Job. We are not struck silent for seven days and nights by Koheleth's condition. Distance is preserved—as is often the case in the comic—between actor and audience. But no resolution is attained. The disjunction between the human situation and the cosmos is not resolved in harmony or life or peace. Throughout, the note of vanity that characterizes all is sounded again and again. Thus, the Book of Koheleth speaks more about determination than about courage. There is the courage here neither to dare to challenge nor even to reach out to the savage god. Nor is there the faith to await the benevolent working out of the mysterious ways of a just and loving deity who "means it for good." Here, at best, is grim determination to live in a world without contact with this deity. Koheleth can play with the idea of release in death and even toy with the thought of never having been born (4:2–3; 6:3–5), but it is idle speculation. He is no Saul!

In a way not even characteristic of the Book of Job or the tragedy of King Saul, Koheleth stands outside the Hebraic tradition. His vision of the deity offers potential for the tragic vision, but the human stance it adopts in the face of this vision prevents its attaining fruition. In this, we gain a new perspective on something that the tragic vision and more normative Hebraic traditions have in common: in both, the deity is active in this cosmos and in the lives of human beings within it. The issue is the nature of that divine action and how it correlates with the best of the imaginations of the human heart. But an inactive deity—or one that at best scatters a few crumbs of momentary pleasure in the way of humans to keep them content in their busy work as they walk the path toward death—calls neither for the faith of a Samuel, a David, or a Joseph, nor for the determination to realize all that human potential offers: the voice of a determined Saul or a Job.

NOTES

1. See, e.g., Frye, *Great Code,* 156, 169, 176.
2. See above, 49–50.
3. The juxtaposition of Koheleth with the Song of Songs in one way or another in our Bible balances another sort of passion with the generally dispassionate tone of the former.
4. Dealing with the herding or eating or striving for the wind *(reˁût rûªh).*
5. J. L. Crenshaw points to a fine if bitter humor in such units as 4:9–12 and 9:4–5 ("The Shadow of Death in Qoheleth," in *Israelite Wisdom: Theological and Literary Essays in Honor of Samuel Terrien,* ed. J. G. Gammie, et al. (Missoula, Mont.: Scholars Press, 1978), 205–16.
6. See R. Gordis, *Koheleth: The Man and His World* (New York: Schocken Books, 1968); J. L. Crenshaw, "The Eternal Gospel (Eccl. 3:11)" in *Essays in Old Testament Ethics: J. Phillip Hyatt in Memoriam,* ed. J. L. Crenshaw and J. T. Willis (New York: KTAV, 1974), 23–55.
7. Crenshaw, "The Shadow of Death."
8. The phrase is used by E. Becker in his introduction to *Denial of Death,* ix.

CHAPTER 7

A Time and a Season
for the Tragic Vision

We have observed on more than one occasion that the Hebraic tradition did not provide fertile soil for the sustained development of the tragic vision. In fact, when one steps back to take in the broader sweep of the Western cultural tradition, it is apparent that the tragic vision developed in a most uneven, indeed, in a sporadic manner. While a few periods and places seem attuned to this vision, able and even driven to attain it, others seem doomed—in spite of the best efforts by otherwise consummate literary artists—to fall short.[1] It is a human trait to attempt the characterization and schematization of human history, and all schemes will stand judged by the complexity and ambiguity of particular periods. Nevertheless, it is striking that it was Athens of the fifth century B.C.E., or England in the Elizabethan age, or late nineteenth- and early twentieth-century America that witnessed full literary flowerings of the tragic vision. Not that there were no individuals who produced works of remarkable tragic strength at other times and places; but these particular periods and places seem to be characterized by a sustained development of the tragic vision. While we must not oversimplify and cannot enter into detail here, what broadly characterizes these ages is that they stood suspended between the more or less dramatic breakup of older and long-enduring patterns of thought and action and the emergence of new patterns to replace them.

These prove to be periods of both intense excitement and deep-seated dread. Old beliefs, old traditions, old customs were fundamentally called into question. In each period, that which defined and identified a culture and sustained life fell in the eyes of many before challenges from the forces of nature, the thrusts of history, and the impulses and imaginations of human beings. Many found themselves cast adrift or hurled into the turbulence of violent seas of chaos, with no point of reference, no bearings, no prospect of a secure landing. The old curtain of culture was pulled back for a moment, and a glimpse of primal terrors become too apparent for many to avoid. Basic questions burnt once again. Some people clung to the older patterns with a grim determination that resulted in clever but desperate mockery of the new waves (witness the plays of Aristophanes in fifth-century Athens) or even with a fierceness that destroyed not only what it opposed but itself as well (the same Athens destroyed its finest flower in Socrates). Others delighted in the fall of the old and the discomfort it brought—Socrates pointed to some who took delight when he showed how hollow the reputed wise men of his day were—but did not stay to engage in the hard work of building new structures on the ruins of the old. A few saw the fall of the old as the challenge and occasion for a new creation. It was before the powerful constructs and images of those we call the pre-Socratics and then of Socrates that the old traditions and values fell, and upon them Plato and Aristotle, among others, were able to build new structures that would help shape Western culture for centuries.

There emerges a dialectic between the destructive and the creative, between the breakup of one world and the formation of another, between the old and the new, that characterizes broadly these points at which tragedy found sustained articulation and development. In the interface between the poles of this dialectic, fundamental questions force themselves upon us—questions human beings rarely find the need or courage to ask, let alone answer, with more than the tried and true. What does it mean to be a man or a woman? What limits are placed by gods or nature on being human? What does it mean for a man or woman "to be"? What is the nature of this cosmos in which we must realize this being, and what is our relationship as creature to the creator and sustainer of this cosmos? In one way, these questions are always asked by certain men and women, but generally only with ready answers near at hand, answers that sustain and comfort. But at a few *kairotic* points, the course of human history is such that these answers are shattered, and in the course of the search for new answers, some struggle with the prospect of even more terrifying possibilities: that the gods are savage; that the cosmos is little attuned to the strivings of human hearts; that the best of us live in deadly tension between the realities of our situation and our imaginations of what might be, between possibilities of justice, divine service, goodness, peace, and blessing, and senseless suffering and death.

It can be suggested that the age of Hammurabi of Babylon, to which the oldest form of the full *Gilgamesh Epic* can be ascribed, was of this type. Through the military and political skills and the ruthlessness of its ruler, Mesopotamia emerged under his leadership from a period of turbulence and darkness united once more and with new cultural, social, and legal visions. We cannot go into detail here, for materials are thin at points, but it is quite possible that it was in this period that new prospects for human being were envisioned, at least for the few who rose above others. No longer simply "robots" or lowly servants (like Job of the folk tale) of largely incomprehensible deities whose only demand was for unquestioning allegiance and submission, some dared to dream and even demand more from the cosmos. A code of law implied patterns of justice in the cosmos, and knowable patterns at that. Humans needed no longer fear the gods for nought. New intimations of human potential, new possibilities for human initiative, and new responsibility for the formulation and definition of their own lives became apparent. The potential for human construction of its own being seemed, if not infinite, at least beyond anything conceived in the past. What were the limits on human being? Who defined the boundaries? What were the implications and costs in heroic exploration of new possibilities and responsibilities that sparked the imaginations of some? It was within this complex nexus of questions that *The Gilgamesh Epic* took shape, as it sought to explore the appeal of territories never before charted by humankind, taking its hero to the boundaries and then beyond even the waters of death. Gilgamesh was no robot, and the position assigned human being reflected in the *Enuma elish* could not be his. In time, only immortality would do for him, even as he knew that "only the gods live forever under the sun." This disjunction between the strivings of a heroic human being and the fixed nature of a cosmos in which death is humankind's fate brings Gilgamesh to the brink of success and then on to tragic defeat. In his fall, we catch sight for a moment of new vistas of human potential as well as clear demarcation of mortal boundaries. His struggle for immortality means we can never be the same. The figure of Gilgamesh is at once a challenge and a warning, and to ignore either or both is to brutalize oneself and one's world.[2]

As we turn to the Hebraic world, we find that the two most extensive developments of the tragic vision, along with several further flirtations with it, group themselves roughly about two crises in the life of old Israel. The first coincides with the formation of the empire which David and then Solomon ruled for less than a century from newly captured Jerusalem. The second is sparked by the death of the last remains of old Israel as a nation with the destruction of Jerusalem in 587 B.C.E. by the armies of Nebuchadnezzar II. It is widely recognized that these two periods share significantly in just those fundamental characteristics that define those rare seasons and settings that prove fertile for the sustained development of the tragic vision. With the work of David and Solomon, a fundamental transformation of Israel on every level of its life was effected. It was a period at once creative and destructive, with the scales tipped according to one's perspective. Old patterns and values gave way to new. An empire reaching from Egypt to the Euphrates—in commercial and cultural influence if not in military might—replaced a federation of loosely united peoples barely hanging onto often marginal land in southern Palestine. Horizons expanded dramatically, and a pluralism in religious and cultural traditions characterized especially the royal city of Jerusalem. Local centers of older power and tradition came into the shadow of the expanding city on the hill. We have already considered some of the dynamics of this,[3] and it must be recognized that it took centuries to come to grips with the implications of what took place. Perspectives and evaluations were divided on many interconnected lines. Serious initial attempts were launched to confront human issues in this *kairotic* moment and to set forth new perspectives on human being, its limits and potential, its powers and responsibilities, and its relation to the cosmos and creator. It is in this context that we set the old tragedy of King Saul that stands buried in the present form of 1 Samuel. It is also in this period that the Yahwist appropriated and recast materials from his Near Eastern environment quite likely new to Israel (e.g., the stories of Eden, of Cain and Abel, and possibly that of the near sacrifice of Isaac)—materials that toy, if fleetingly, with the tragic. Certainly, by this time, a basic collection of traditions about Samson had taken shape.

As traumatic and provocative as was the death of the ancient nation of Israel in 587,[4] this was a second crisis both destructive and yet constructive; again, one's particular perspective would qualify the assessment. Institutions and symbols, as well as myths and patterns of worship that infused them with sacred meaning, were shattered. Yet from the debris of the old new patterns and institutions, new stories, songs, and rites would arise. The life of Jeremiah took in both the last days of Israel and the death of his nation. The Book of Job arose in the decades immediately after 587 among those in exile in the east.

Once again, it was a time and season for the tragic vision, even in a Hebraic tradition that had demonstrated earlier in its treatment of the tragedy of King Saul just how difficult it was for that vision to sustain a foothold. Once more, the facade of sometimes hard-won and sometimes glib affirmations of Yahweh's justice and/or love were stripped away, and an original terror and abyss loomed into the consciousness of those unable simply to sit and weep, who could no longer remember Jerusalem in the old ways, who could no longer sing the old songs of Zion.

Out of destruction, new creations sometimes arise; out of shattered beliefs and patterns for life may spring in time new modes for thinking and feeling and acting. Out of this dialectic between the old and the new arises the tragic vision. M. Krieger has spoken of tragedy as *agent provocateur*, testing the depth of the old and new assumptions of a time and place.[5] It exists as a challenge to all attempts, in the face of what has fallen, to hang onto or flirt with easy answers, cheap grace, glib assertions, or a middle way. It does not offer a developed philosophy or theology or new religious way. It is more elemental, defining the ground and staking out the full extent and limits of the stage upon which new ways and patterns will have to be played out. It goes behind the old ways and dogmas to the most basic terrors emerging from a primal confrontation between human being and the cosmic forces that define the context in which we struggle "to be." Its roots are set in the most ancient of human terrors: fears that in spite of all human efforts in word and deed, in myth and ritual, chaos will not give way to cosmos, death will not revolve in a cycle with life, life-giving flood or rains will fail, and starvation and pestilence will seize the hardened earth in a final grip. Tragedy makes clear that dreams of freedom and promise can emerge only out of the terrors of slavery and the radical dislocation of wandering in the wilderness. In this, it reaches out beyond both old and new to set forth visions of heroic human strivings and the cost these efforts exact. It certifies that resurrection can only follow crucifixion. Only in facing the full force of the tragic potential in the life and death of King Saul can one dare go on to assert, with Joseph, that with time and a broad perspective on the human situation one can see "God meant it for good." Only after one faces the struggles and terrors and suffering of Job can one dream of a new exodus, a new Zion, a new covenant, a new heaven and earth, let alone declare with Ezekiel that the deity's dealings with each individual human being are commensurate with the moral quality of his or her life and are tempered by a desire to bless. "Tragedy," says N. Frye, "reflects the human situation as it is, and comedy normally attains its happy ending through some mysterious and unexpected twist in the plot."[6] The sudden and mysterious are prime characteristics of the god of the Hebraic tradition, often in the service of just the sort of resolution that defines high comedy. The brief glimpses of the tragic vision highlight this dimension of our heritage.

Reality is held in its harshest light by the tragic vision, not primarily to shatter old illusions and aspirations—for these have usually already been shown to be fundamentally flawed, even if some people still cling to them with a last gasp of desperation—but to challenge the new that is emerging. It was their deep-seated inability to face the human situation represented by the man named Job that made crass the orthodox assertions of his friends and won for them the epitaph "miserable comforters" (Job 16:2). Indeed, the Book of Job remains in the canon as a work of questions, in which the answer of the deity from the storm is, as we have seen, a non sequitur that calls into question all human questions asked of him and all answers offered.

While it is the harsh human situation that tragedy holds before us— Job on his ash heap, Saul in the cave at Endor and on the heights of Gilboa—tragedy also sets before us a perspective on the cosmos that places the human being at the periphery: "Where were you when I created the heavens and the earth?" From this perspective on the edge of the cosmos and not at the center, the ways and wills of the gods must appear to human beings as at times arbitrary, unreasoning, unjust—indeed, savage. Off-center, human beings can center the universe about themselves only through a life of illusion. Tragic heroes have their illusions, but grand illusions characteristic of the tragic hero are also a drive for reality that will not allow illusion to stand. Oedipus will have the truth; Gilgamesh will not deviate from his quest by being lulled by the commonplace; Saul will act as king and serve his people and deity; Job will deny neither his own integrity nor all that has happened to him. The tragic hero will not easily skew his drive for reality in order to allow the illusion of human centeredness to remain. Thus, Job and his friends begin with the same principles, but while the three will not depart from them even in the face of the reality that is Job, he must abandon them as he seeks to remain true to who he is, what he has become, and the god behind his image of god. The striving to bring illusion and reality together is shown in time by the gods to be destructive, but a destruction that is unique to the tragic hero. Other mortals fall back quickly, living their illusions through the sometimes brutal denial of reality (e.g., that by Eliphaz and his companions), trusting that a "mysterious and unexpected twist in the plot" will turn potentially tragic reality into comedy ("God meant it for good"), or standing back from both illusion and reality with a bemused if bitter smile, taking what bits of enjoyment come their way and intellectualizing (Koheleth).

The tragic vision offers not a philosophy or a theology—it does not stake out a way or a system. As *agent provocateur*, it is a stone in the path: a stone over which those who cling in futile desperation to the old must stumble; a stone that will trip up those who seek to construct new visions in too facile a way. It can also be a stone that some will take up and incorporate into the edifice they build; for among human beings there will be no end to the making of philosophies and theologies, systems and dogmas, structures and symbol systems. There must not be. Those humans who will endure for more than a season, those who will sustain life through generations and not just for a day or week or year, will be those who have been able to take up the stone that is the tragic vision—as with the Christian's cross or the Jew's bondage in Egypt and in exile—and set it as the cornerstone for their structure. Thus, it is a too often neglected strength of the Hebraic tradition—neglected to the detriment of those religious traditions fed by its roots—that while generally so uncongenial to the tragic vision with its heroic human being and savage god, the tragic does make an appearance at certain times and seasons and cannot be wholly denied. Efforts to skew or blunt the tragedy of King Saul were not wholly successful, and the complex process of tradition that in time gave shape to 1 Samuel could not obscure from the sensitive reader the tragic vision, even when set in layers of prophetic and royalist affirmations.[7] The Book of Job, with its unanswered and unanswerable questions upon questions, remains in some arrangements of the canon (the LXX and those that follow it) literally at the center.[8] And this is apt, in spite of scholarship's treatment of Job as peripheral to the Hebraic tradition even if it is of great depth in its own right; for it is the position of this book that makes the canon a critique as well as a guide, a challenge as well as a comfort, affirming the human being even as it declares the human's limits, facing the tragic even as it transcends it.

The Hebraic tradition did not produce tragedy in any sustained way or much material informed by the tragic vision. But at their best, expressions of that tradition had behind them intimations of the tragic. Ancient Israelite traditions and the Jewish, Christian, and Islamic traditions built upon them all transcend the tragic. Promise fulfilled and to be fulfilled transcends exile and alienation; freedom won and to be won transcends bondage; resurrection accomplished and to be accomplished lift us out of the valley of death; hope overcomes suffering. Tragedy is transcended but not skirted. As in the case of the Book of Job, we pass through the tragic vision to new affirmations of the human being in relation to new visions and experiences of the deity. The savage god of the tragic vision is not finally the god of the Hebraic tradition. But visions of a just god that were rooted in prophetic circles were built in part from confrontation with the dread power of the tragedy of King Saul. The vision of the loving father whose embrace takes in all humanity found early formulation in Davidic circles that took up the tragedy of King Saul as well. Circles centering on the figures of Samuel and David did not simply ignore the old tragedy; they recast it and even blunted its force, but in so doing they also had to face it. When some were no longer willing to face it, these later spokesmen for an orthodoxy became rigid and stood condemned in the figures of Job's three friends. The justice and love that informed the actions of the god of the Hebraic heritage were rarely cheap, and sporadic but intense confrontations with the tragic vision helped insure this.

Clearly, the challenge posed by this stone that is the tragic vision still lies in our religious paths and needs to be faced today as always— quite likely as never before, with this century's overwhelming evidence of the demonic powers within human being and of the holocausts without that arise from them. The sometimes harsh reality of the human situation that the tragic vision holds out is a needed judgment and critique upon all the glib pseudoreligious systems that crowd the shelves of popular book stores and even our not-so-super- markets—systems as flimsy and insubstantial as the paper and binding of the booklets that contain them, but that entice with the power of illusion and seduce us with false clarity of single issues and solutions for our political, personal, social, and economic problems. The realities of oppression, brutalization, torture, and hunger that strip human lives of integrity or drive human beings to assert their integrity with their flesh in their teeth must not be hidden by slick mass communications, glimmering edifices of glass and steel, or pretty bells. The fears that lie in each of us, that can be tapped at any moment by events that stand beyond our control and even our understanding (a child's senseless death, a plane plummeting from the sky, a mortar shell fired by forces that seem unable to care less, a life's work and hope destroyed by an economy out of control): these fears cannot be allowed to fester under a thin if glowing coat of cheap affirmations and false comfort that can only lead to shallow lives or lives warped and made grotesque by pain unfaced and unexpressed. This suffering aspect of humanity is recalled in the suffering of the tragic hero.

There is another aspect as well. In human context, where the power to move minds and mountains, tap the powers of the atom, and reach out to the stars tempts some of us to center the cosmos about us in ways that make the older assertions of a human- and earth-centered universe seem simple-minded, the challenge of a perspective that places us at the periphery and points out the cost of attempts to shift the center to the periphery must be faced. Job would finally tell us, for example, that our oil deposits are the result of ages of natural processes whose end is not the provision of fuel to feed our unending and wasteful appetite for mobility and heated or cooled air. To live as if this were the sole purpose of nature's design is to court a fall, hints of which are noted even now in our costs and forcibly reduced styles of living, costs that must fall even more heavily on those who will come after us. Visions of a world governed on our model, a world made "safe for democracy," visions often held and implemented with the best intentions, can become destructive cancers in the life of a nation when held with a fierceness that is single-minded and open to no judgment. We cannot make the world over into our image, however grand we may believe that image to be. The illusions of tragic heroes are grand illusions, but they especially must be shattered by the realities of a god-centered and not human-centered cosmos if they become the basis for attempts to move from the periphery to the center—or, godlike, to rebuild the cosmos around us. Saul, Job, Oedipus, and even Adam and Eve sought what we value, and Cain also sought to worship his god. Few of our ideals and deeds will approach the greatness of the tragic heroes, but like theirs, ours must stand under judgment as well, not just with regard to their content but to what we would do and make of them. In an age like ours, that lives too often under illusions that serve the denial of death yet produces death on a scale never imagined before, we must recognize that death is that point where the best of human imaginations comes up against the larger cosmos, centered on powers that are sometimes terrible and always awesome. It is not by chance that each tragic hero's encounter with and recognition of limits is in some way an encounter with death.

On the other hand, the challenge that the tragic vision offers in its depiction of the heroic potential in human being, in the fallen but honored Saul, in the silenced but affirmed Job, is also necessary in a world where too many slip easily into a simple skepticism that can slide into pessimism and despair or anesthetization of all feeling. The tragic hero is precisely human being at its heroic, if flawed, best, seeking the good and the just in a savage world. This image of the human is needed in a world enticed by all sorts of avenues to cop out or dull the senses with easy highs. Not least, the sense of the tragic calls for the finest modes of artistic expression, an aesthetic as compelling as its subject. The simple but many-faceted structure of the tragedy of King Saul, the rhetorical strength of the Book of Job— these stand in sharp judgment on the drab and commonplace that fills so much of life today. Tragedy moves beyond the pretty to essential literary and artistic forms that fuse deep beauty with truth. In a human-made world that is too often as drab and inert as a skyline formed by masses of little block houses with antennas that transmit empty words to the bored fold within, hearing a requiem by Beethoven, watching a production of *Medea*, seeing *The Pietà*, can be profoundly transforming. It has been the vision of the tragic that has called forth the simplest yet grandest expressions of the human spirit, certifying the aesthetic as a vital dimension of human being. This *agent provocateur* enriches lives even as it unsettles them.

Most of all, the tragic vision must inform all attempts to come to terms with holocaust, be it the systematic destruction of over six million Jews in Europe, the endless destruction of the lives of people native to or shipped into Southeast Asia, the incineration of cities with destructive power beyond imagination, the sending of wave after wave of human beings into battles for a few yards of desert or forbidding rock, or the systematic ignorance and calculated denial of the starvation of masses on this earth. For many the European holocaust—the destruction of millions of Jews—has become archetypal of all this. (I write on the eve of the fiftieth year after the first politically organized and legitimized attack on Jews in Germany.) Writers like Elie Wiesel, with a rare strength, have kept before us the vision of that horror with clear indications of the tragic potential realized in the lives of the many who were destroyed and the few who survived. I believe that the tragic vision with its image of the savage god contains the perspectives and challenges needed to focus necessary attempts by Jews, Christians, and all those rooted in the Western heritage to plumb the meaning of that event, each in their own way and from their own perspective of experience, and then perhaps to transcend it. Only the tragic vision can contain the full terror of the holocaust, and only within its perspective can the lives of those caught in it and taken by it burn with a new type of brightness that enlightens and enlarges ours. Only through the tragic vision can the slow journey be made from that long night into the new day.[9] In the face of that holocaust and others—as the *kairotic* and crisis events of this century—we surely find ourselves in a time and season for the tragic vision.

NOTES

1. Sewall, *Vision of Tragedy*, 3–4.
2. See Jacobsen's assessment of Mesopotamia in the first millennium, *Treasures of Darkness*, 226–39.
3. Chap. 3. See also Humphreys, *Crisis and Story*, chaps. 1–4.
4. See Humphreys, *Crisis and Story*, chaps. 7–9 and references there.
5. Krieger, *The Tragic Vision*, chap. 1.
6. Frye, *Great Code*, 156.
7. Too often this is missed by the preacher, teacher, or theologian, or even biblical scholar; it has been the poet—or literarily sensitive, at any rate—who generally perceived the tragic potential in the figure of Saul. See, most recently, Frye, *Great Code*, 181–82.
8. See ibid., 193–97.
9. The literature on the European holocaust is vast. I have found Y. Bauer's *A History of the Holocaust* (New York: Franklin Watts, 1982) a useful orientation to the patterns of cause and flow of events. J. des Pres's study of *The Survivor* (New York and London: Oxford Univ. Press, 1977) a remarkable tribute to and assessment of the power of the human spirit in the face of hell. The volume by A. Roy and Alice L. Echardt, *Long Night's Journey Into Day: Life and Faith After the Holocaust* (Detroit: Wayne State Univ. Press, 1982), is a provocative attempt to confront the holocaust from the perspective of Christians committed to make what transformations, rejections, and affirmations are necessary in the face of it.

Index of Authors

145

Index of Biblical Passages